ELIMINATING SEXUAL HARASSMENT AT WORK

In memory of Garth Boomer

All power...

ELIMINATING SEXUAL HARASSMENT AT WORK

Carrie Herbert

David Fulton Publishers

London

David Fulton Publishers Ltd
2 Barbon Close, London WC1N 3JX

First published in Great Britain by
David Fulton Publishers 1994

Note: The right of Carrie Herbert to be identified as the author of this work has been
asserted by her in accordance with the Copyright, Designs and Patents Act 1988

Copyright © Carrie Herbert

British Library Cataloguing in Publication Data

A catalogue record for this book is available from the British Library

ISBN 1-85346-320-5

Typeset by the author

Printed in Great Britain by BPC Wheatons, Exeter

CONTENTS

ACKNOWLEDGEMENTS

This book is based on the life at work of many women who have found the courage to tell me of their often traumatic experiences, in informal conversations and at workshops and conferences. I have used their stories to expand my knowledge and understanding of the practice and to illustrate the theory of sexual harassment. I should like to thank them all for their invaluable contribution.

I should also like to thank Ruth Loshak for her help in editing this book, and Clive Gillott for contributing the chapter on taking a case of sexual harassment to an Industrial Tribunal.

Carrie Herbert
Cambridge, April 1994

INTRODUCTION

The Aims of this Book

Sexual harassment is an important issue, and one which is beginning to be taken seriously by organizations of all kinds. Whilst there are laws which prohibit sexual discrimination (and sexual harassment constitutes sex discrimination), there is little practical help on the market for people (whether they be managers, recipients, co-workers or students) to enable them to tackle the problem.

What I aim to do in this book is to present a determined common sense approach to dealing with sexual harassment in organizations. I describe how to enable staff in general to learn about it, to understand why it is detrimental and why it has to be eliminated, and to give them ways of combating it. I address the issue of how to change the behaviour of employees responsible for harassment, as well as help those who are the victim of unwanted sexual attention to do something about it themselves. Solutions to sexual harassment can be informal: telling the perpetrator to go away, for instance; formal, such as invoking the institution's sexual harassment policy; or legalistic, bringing a case to an Industrial Tribunal for example.

Sexual harassment is a serious problem. Perpetrators of this behaviour should not be exonerated with comments like 'boys will be boys'. Awareness raising of all staff will ensure that employees know what the term 'sexual harassment' means, how it will be dealt with in your organization, and what grievance procedure is available for recipients. The writing and implementing of a workable and accessible policy to counter sexual harassment is essential.

No one, it seems, is neutral about sexual harassment. Discussion about it elicits strong and emotional reactions. It is not a comfortable topic to deal with. For these reasons, work will need to be done by trainers and educators to make sure your staff is aware of the

1

conflicting issues it raises. Whether or not they themselves have been victims of this unwanted treatment, they will still have feelings about it. Some may decry it as a feminist issue, consider it a waste of time, a woman-only problem, a problem for gay men, or even no problem at all because 'only young and pretty women get sexually harassed' and 'young "girls" like it anyway'. At the other extreme there are likely to be people in your organization who were sexually harassed in the past in a previous job, at university or school, or may be being harassed now, know colleagues who are recipients or just feel very angry about the way in which the institution has hitherto ignored or mishandled the problem.

Then, of course, there will be people who are afraid they might be accused of being a perpetrator of sexual harassment, others who are not quite sure what it is and become anxious about talking to colleagues in case they are so accused. Some may foresee that discussion of the topic will mean more work, more training, and more meetings, and resent this. Some might be unsure of what behaviour will be expected of them in the future, some don't want others to find out that they are or have been victims, fearing that the whole process of training will expose their secret and make it all the more difficult for them and their partner to live their private lives. All these are normal and usual feelings to experience, which need to be acknowledged and defused as effectively and as quickly as possible. But this must be done with care and sensitivity. Managers or training personnel will need information and advice on how to do this, if the organization is to take a responsible attitude towards its employees and the professional health of its workforce.

Ignoring sexual harassment, sweeping it under the carpet, forbidding any discussion, displaying 'old-fashioned patriarchal' reactions to incidents, handling cases which do emerge in an inept way, will all have a devastating effect on the workplace and workforce. Interpersonal relations will be sullied by mistrust and dishonesty. Work productivity and efficiency will drop. The result of mishandling a complaint may even result in a long drawn-out sex discrimination case if one of the employees decides to take legal action.

If one looks at the seats of power and influence, one sees that the governing, policing, military, legal, medical, religious, educational and financial bodies in the UK up to now have predominantly been directed by men. It is unsurprising therefore that they overwhelmingly conform to male attitudes and suit male ways of working. This helps to explain why sexual harassment is very much more of a problem for women as recipients and a way of behaving for men as harassers. But whilst it is a problem for women, it is not just a woman's issue; it is one that men and women must tackle together.

This book gives essential background reading, surveys the basic arguments and presents necessary information for effective and valid training. I have written it in conjunction with *Countering Sexual Harassment: A Training Pack*, published by Daniels Publishing of Cambridge. The pack, which is available separately, provides activities, questions, ideas for role-plays and small and large group discussions, and methods of presentation for personnel trainers and human resources managers.

Each of the fourteen chapters of the book deals with a specific aspect of sexual harassment. For example, if you want information about how to write and implement a policy, Chapter 6: Writing and Implementing a Sexual Harassment Policy, will help you do this. If you need information on how to train managers, and employees, or on some of the principles that should be followed when dealing with harassers, each of these topics is dealt with under the appropriately named chapter.

For you to be able to access the information you require quickly some of it is repeated because it is relevant in more than one chapter. For example, in one chapter the common misconceptions concerning sexual harassment are challenged, and in another a manager is alerted to the types of excuses and reasons an alleged harasser might give for harassing behaviour. The responses for each of these are similar because one of the best known defences of the sexual harasser is that the recipient has sought it out, enjoyed it or provoked it, whereas I would suggest that the stated wishes of the person who is the object of the behaviour are of paramount importance in determining whether or not the behaviour in dispute is wanted or not. Or, when defending his behaviour, the harasser may say he didn't mean it like that, he was only being friendly. This raises the question: what role does intention play in deciding a case of sexual harassment and does it matter what his intentions were? You will find that intention is referred to in several other chapters.

Information is given on the role management must play in countering sexual harassment, what the law says, what the cost to an organization might be for ignoring or dealing ineptly with a case of sexual harassment, and how to respond to a recipient who comes to you for help. There is also a chapter containing statistics on sexual harassment.

During the course of this guide, where the sex of a person is specified I refer to the harasser as *he*. This is because the vast majority of people who perpetrate sexual harassment are men. By the same token, I usually refer to recipients as women. This is not to deny that there are some men whose life is made uncomfortable, are embarrassed and humiliated by the unwanted sexual attention of a woman colleague. There are male homosexuals who are subject to sexual harassment, too. But the advice and activities suggested for recipients can be used with little adaptation to suit any recipient, whether female or male, gay or straight. Similarly, whether the harasser is a man or a woman, gay or straight, the advice given in this book on how to deal with them applies equally across the board.

CHAPTER ONE

Putting Sexual Harassment in Context

Introduction

In the last decade sexual harassment has become one of the most
talked about issues of the workplace, bursting into our sitting rooms
from America via the case brought by Anita Hills against Clarence
Thomas, and in Britain, by Dr Malcolm Smith claiming that he had
been slandered by Dr Alanah Houston. In neither case was the
woman's claim of harassment upheld, but this did not damp down the
issue: rather it fuelled and fanned the flames, challenging the view that
sexual harassment was just a part of work life and as such 'normal'
behaviour.

The role of consciousness raising

There are many reasons for the growing debate and concern about
sexual harassment at work. Renewed and broader interest in women's
rights was sparked off in the 1960s in this country. During that decade
there was the introduction of the contraceptive pill, legislation which
decriminalized abortion (Abortion Act, 1967) and a phenomenon
called *Consciousness Raising*, imported into the UK from the United
States.

Consciousness raising did what its name suggests. It raised the
general awareness of women, bringing the subject of women's issues
into the homes and lives of ordinary women, many of them
housewives. In houses all round the country, all-women meetings were
held on a variety of levels. The discussions engendered at the meetings
gave women a political dimension and a critical view of their individual

positions as wives and mothers. Also, and importantly, they gave women a deeper, collective understanding of how women as a group had been consistently and systematically discriminated against because they were women.

The strategy of providing a forum for women to discuss issues that interested them, in an all-woman environment, broke into the traditionally narrow sphere of a woman's life. When married, she was expected to be a loyal and uncritical supporter of her husband and at the same time silent about her own needs, especially if that need was one of loneliness. Women who participated in the groups took the time to talk about their personal predicament to other group members. They were alerted to the realization that other women were in similar positions. They made space to discuss and explore their feeling that staying at home and raising children was not totally satisfying or fulfilling. They made use of the opportunity to share their isolation and their feelings of hopelessness. This made them realize that the valium they had been taking was not going to help them counteract the boredom they felt, the underuse of their minds and intellect, or the fact that their status derived purely from the position of their husband or their children's achievements.

In the consciousness-raising groups women achieved an understanding and perception of themselves as part of a much larger situation, in which most women were without independent financial means and without personal power and autonomy; in which most women had no opportunity for a career due to the lack of childcare facilities, their lack of education and training, as well as their husbands' reluctance to allow them to work and the social pressures which argued strongly that a woman's place was in the home.

Catherine Hall argues that this period gave women the opportunity to understand that sexual politics, 'the politics of power relations between men and women', was part of everyday personal life. She went on to say that this new awareness brought with it questions regarding the division of domestic labour. Who was responsible for and did the washing up, who changed the nappies, who swept the floor and who did the shopping? It also raised the uncomfortable question about who felt it was their fault when things went wrong in the family or household. The conclusions which were drawn by women in these groups soon indicated that the predicament of women was not just to do with individual difficulties between couples but that it was part of the social organization of power (Hall, 1992, p.15).

By making the 'personal the political' in this way women became more autonomous, more confident, more aware of their position. This in turn provided them with confidence to take action.

The Sex Discrimination Act (1975) and the changes that the Equal Opportunities Commission encouraged, supported the female cause and provided a public platform from which women could voice their opinions and ideas. It also raised women's expectations so that they began to seek and demand careers with professional and managerial responsibilities. The 1960s and 70s were years in which there was a growing general awareness of workplace rights and employer responsibilities, especially in the area of women's rights.

The naming of sexual harassment

It was in the rapidly changing workplace environment in the US that the issue of unwanted sexual attention was first named. In 1974, in her research on Women and Work at Cornell University, Lin Farley turned to the strategy of consciousness raising, 'a remarkable tool for unlocking the vast storehouse of knowledge, women's own experiences'. Lin Farley wrote:

> Our first 'C-R' session was devoted to work, and my students and I determined at the outset to discipline ourselves to focus on what had happened to us on our jobs because we were women. As we each took our turn speaking, I was a peer; the group was a nearly equal division of black and white, with economic backgrounds ranging from very affluent to poor. Still, when we had finished, there was an unmistakable pattern to our employment. Something absent in all the literature, something I had never seen although I had observed it many times, was newly exposed. Each one of us had already quit or been fired from a job at least once because we had been made too uncomfortable by the behavior of men... The male behavior eventually required a name, and *sexual harassment* seemed to come about as close to symbolizing the problem as the language would permit. (Farley, 1978, pp.11-12).

Of course, sexual harassment had been in existence prior to Lin Farley's naming of it. A statement made in the seventeenth century: 'It is not becoming in a person of quality in the company of ladies, to handle them roughly: to put his hand in their necks or bosoms: to kiss them by surprise: to force their letters or books from them: to look into their papers etc.' (The Rules of Civility, Anon, 1695), is a clear indication that some men did put their 'hands in women's bosoms', and thought it all right to do so.

Individual women had experienced negative, humiliating and embarrassing behaviour from male colleagues, friends and employers but had not been able to speak out about it because they didn't know what to call it. It could be argued that one of the reasons that sexual harassment remained invisible and undetected at a public level was that, first, it was behaviour that men did not experience as victims in any great numbers, at all frequently or severely and, second, that the behaviour women found offensive was described by men as flattering, friendly, normal, just a joke or a bit of a laugh.

Once sexual harassment had a name, there followed a plethora of research projects which set out to find the true extent of this 'new' problem (see Chapter 4: Statistics). *Redbook*, a women's radical magazine, conducted research in 1976. The United Nations Ad Hoc Group on Equal Rights for Women committee made a similar study in 1981. In Britain, the National and Local Government Officers Association (NALGO) and the Alfred Marks Bureau conducted research in 1982 to ascertain the extent to which sexual harassment occurred and the effects it had on those who were its victims. However, this was not a straightforward process. Once sexual harassment was defined it became evident that there were problems fitting all women's experiences into the chosen definitions because of the confusion about what was 'normal' behaviour for men, and what was not. There was also the problem of the differing thresholds individual women had, for what was considered acceptable behaviour by one was not necessarily acceptable to another. However, there was no longer a question of whether sexual harassment existed, for that had been established, but there was a problem distinguishing it from acceptable sexual behaviour, given the sexual traditions of Western society.

Trade unions and other bodies

In the early 1980s, when they became aware of the detrimental effect this behaviour had on their women members, forward-looking unions began to address the issue of sexual harassment and published pamphlets and brochures to bring the problem into the open.

In July 1981, NALGO issued guidelines on combating sexual harassment at work. The pamphlet incorporated a leaflet entitled

Sexual harassment is a trade union issue which described the unwanted behaviour and gave a six-point plan for fighting harassment. The 1982 Trades Union Congress (TUC) Women's Conference carried a resolution on sexual harassment, recognising it as a form of sexual discrimination which could damage a woman's morale, job security and prospects at work. They defined it as 'repeated and unwanted verbal or sexual advances, sexually derogatory statements or sexually discriminating remarks' (TUC, 1983, p.3).

The National Council for Civil Liberties (NCCL) published a booklet and defined sexual harassment as ranging from patronizing language to unwanted sexual behaviours. They gave examples of women who said it was: putting his hand up my skirt, a pin-up of a woman with her legs wide open, blowing down the neck of a woman's jumper and a remark such as 'your nipples are sticking out' (Sedley & Benn, 1982, pp. 3-12).

Whilst at one level women and unions were challenging companies, organizations and education establishments to deal with it effectively, so managers were becoming aware that sexual harassment had major implications for productivity, efficiency and staff turnover. Employers, realising that sexual harassment could have a detrimental effect on the performance of everyone in the workplace and an effect on production levels, began to look more closely at their equal opportunity policies and, in particular, the inclusion in it of a section on sexual harassment.

In the 1990s more and more organizations are coming to realize that they need sexual harassment policies and grievance procedures in order to protect their workers and cover themselves. It is also clear that managers understand that there is a great need for training and development in this area. Details on how to devise a useful and worthwhile policy, and how to implement it successfully, are given in Chapter 6.

The difficulty with defining sexual harassment

How men perceive certain behaviours that women deem to be sexual harassment reflects two totally different truths. In many cases neither party is lying. Nor is the difference in perception between men and women the only factor. Women and girls experience such a wide range of situations in which sexually harassing behaviour takes place, that it is difficult to adequately encompass all their experiences in a definition. Furthermore, the way in which women and girls perceive a particular behaviour depends on their education, social conditioning, maturity, sexual experience and political awareness, making it all the more difficult to find a generic description.

One of the problems associated with defining and naming sexual harassment is that for many, both men and women, the list of behaviours encompassed in the term can also meet the criteria for what our society sees as 'normal' and, in many situations, desired behaviour. The difference lies in the context: in the interpretation and the experiences of the people involved, the time/location of the behaviour and the relationship/status of those concerned. Pursuit of a partner is engaged in by the majority of people and is encouraged and considered natural and 'normal'. The rules of how to play the 'mating game' however, are fairly specific and sex-stereotyped. The man is the 'hunter', the woman the 'prey' and certain codes of behaviour decide how each sex will play their part. The parts allocated to each sex provide a fertile ground in which sexual harassment can occur.

Sexual harassment: the chameleon

If we are aware of what constitutes consensual sexual behaviour between consenting adults in the workplace, surely it is possible to know what behaviour is not mutually acceptable? Why is it that there seems to be a confusion between friendly behaviour and sexual harassment?

When a couple are engaged in a consensual sexual relationship, their communication involves a wide variety of different behaviours which may be observed by outsiders. These include: wolf-whistles, pats, strokes, nudges, cuddles, winks, nods, kisses, repeated requests for dates, sexual innuendoes about clothes, body size, hair, leisure and weekend activities, presents, sexual jokes and *double entendres*. Couples who behave like this are considered 'normal'. However, this same behaviour becomes a very different experience if disliked by one of the parties. They may feel used, harassed, or even abused. Unfortunately, if this person is the woman, and she raises a protest, she is sometimes seen by outsiders, or the harasser himself, as playing hard to get, being frigid, humourless, a flirt or a prick-tease, or just a difficult and a stupid woman.

Unfortunate, too, is the attitude that even if the woman finds the behaviour offensive, the man is often excused responsibility for causing distress with comments along the lines that it is acceptable for the man to behave like this because it is both 'normal' and 'natural', he is 'only trying it on', or that he is being a 'real man', or a 'boy being a boy'.

So in some situations a man may make a sexual advance to a woman and it constitutes consensual behaviour, and in another situation the same behaviour may be construed by the recipient as sexual harassment. A difficult dilemma!

Unfortunately in many workplace settings it is still unacceptable for women to complain either personally or publicly. The sexual attention/sexual harassment dilemma is usually seen from the point of view of the man and his intentions, his personal standing and status supporting him against the woman's complaints which are seen as hysterical, exaggerated and misplaced. However, personal testimonies from a large number of women who have left positions of employment show that they are victims of sexual harassment in such diverse places as shops, boardrooms, factories, law courts, schools, the street, universities, trains and buses, leisure centres – in short, wherever women and men meet and communicate.

CHAPTER TWO

Defining Sexual Harassment

Introduction

I indicated in the previous chapter that there are problems with defining sexual harassment because of its chameleon-like qualities. Whether certain behaviour constitutes sexual harassment or not is dependent on the recipient naming it as unwanted. This makes sexual harassment highly subjective, causing confusion for many people. In some cases a hug, a wink, being called 'love' or being told a sexist joke is sexual harassment and, in another context, or with another person, the very same behaviour is welcomed and reciprocated.

So what is it about some behaviour which makes it sexual harassment? It must be clear from the beginning that behaviour which is unwanted and which is detrimental to a person's ability to do their job effectively, whatever we end up calling it, must be stopped. It must also be recognized that a person has the right to say, and must be given encouragement to say: 'I don't like this; it makes me feel uncomfortable'. At the same time it is incumbent on employers to encourage their employees to become more aware of colleagues' tolerances, individual likes and dislikes and the standard of behaviour that the workplace demands.

Unwanted sexual attention

The first criterion, then, for behaviour to be called sexual harassment is that it is unwanted. Everyone is unique; people expect different amounts of personal space, have different tolerances to touches, pats and hugs, and these differences need to be accommodated. This means that touching people without their express wish can no longer be regarded as ok behaviour, or as 'only being friendly'. You may like to touch others and be touched by them; but that does not mean that everyone else will. Similarly, just because someone has always assumed that they could pat or stroke or hug a particular person, and that person hasn't seemed to mind, it doesn't mean they don't mind, or that they should continue to behave in that way from now on without checking it out. Perhaps, if you are a man, before you touch or hug someone, you should ask yourself some questions:

- Why am I doing this?

- Am I hugging/touching this person because she is - a woman?

- Is she senior or junior to me, or is she of equal status?

- Am I in a position to fire her, or have her dismissed?

- Does the fact I am older/younger than she is make a difference?

- Would I like this sort of thing to be done to my daughter/wife/sister/mother?

- What would happen if I stopped doing it?

- What would she say if I asked her if she minded?

If we dwell for a few moments on who touches whom and why, we soon realize that it is not juniors who touch seniors, but older, more authoritarian figures who usually pat, stroke and touch their subordinates. A young or new telephonist rarely feels it appropriate to put her arm around her boss's shoulders before telling him that he has been left a message. So it looks as if the power situation has a lot to do with the whole matter.

We know, however, that it is not just touching or hugging that women are subject to. Winks, nods, gestures and *billets doux* can also constitute sexual harassment. These need to be checked out in the same way, by asking yourself the same questions, and examining whether you are in a powerful situation vis-à-vis this person.

Quid pro quo

This brings us to a second major criterion governing whether behaviour can be classed as sexual harassment, namely, that in some way the recipient will be disadvantaged if she refuses the harasser his request, or objects to his attention. In serious cases this conduct is called *quid pro quo*, this for that, one of the main subjects of sexual harassment litigation in the USA. This type of sexual harassment is based on the premise that the recipient will get a pay-off if she comes across sexually: the harasser will make sure that her name goes forward for promotion, she will get a pay rise, she will pass her course, or she is not on the next redundancy list. More often in this country, however, it seems that the spurned sexual harasser invokes reprisals against the victim, demanding that she work harder, criticizing her work and her behaviour and undermining her standing amongst her colleagues.

The characteristics of sexual harassment

Intentional or unintentional?

One of the many problems for people in coming to understand sexual harassment in the workplace is the concept of intentionality. I so often hear the sentiments: 'If the harasser didn't mean it then it can't be sexual harassment'. I'm sorry, but it can and is. Sexual harassment is not based on the intentions of the harasser, but on the feelings and experience of the recipient. It does not matter what the harasser intended. He may have intended to be pleasant, friendly, make her feel at home, cheer her up a bit, and many other similar notions. But the fact remains, if the recipient finds them patronizing, unwanted, embarrassing and unacceptable then they must stop and not be repeated.

The difference between someone who intends to sexually harass and someone who doesn't will emerge at the time of disciplinary procedures. A manager dealing with a perpetrator who is genuinely apologetic, because he had meant to make the woman feel welcome, will be treated differently from a harasser who has no care about the woman's feelings or is reckless as to her wishes.

A defence for a man who unintentionally harasses is not, 'if she didn't like it why didn't she tell me at the time, because I would have stopped'. For example, if the recipient of harassment is a junior clerk and the harasser her line manager, the woman may well feel that she has no rights, her request will not be taken seriously or may itself cause offence, and consequently she doesn't have the confidence to ask him to stop. It can therefore be the case that a perpetrator may be totally unaware that he has sexually harassed a person.

It is thus extremely important to raise men's awareness of what may constitute sexual harassment. This should result in a marked decrease in incidents. The more intractable intentional harassment can then be dealt with.

Direct and indirect sexual harassment

Sexual harassment is usually aimed at one particular person. If the recipient is touched, patted, or asked in person for a date and finds this attention unpleasant, this is *direct* sexual harassment. However, people may be affected indirectly by verbal or physical behaviour at work.

Take, for example, a group of men in an office or staff room discussing the attributes of a page three model in the presence of others who find the comments offensive, judge them to be lewd and obnoxious. Whilst the claim from the men could be: 'We weren't talking to you, you shouldn't have been listening', the fact remains that their behaviour is unwanted, humiliating or offensive and is creating embarrassment for other workers. Behaviour by men which fosters an environment in which women and women's bodies are seen as objects affects 'the dignity of women and men at work', as the EC document on sexual harassment puts it (Rubenstein 1989). This is *indirect* sexual harassment and needs to be stopped.

Naming the behaviour

Now let me return to the first criterion for naming behaviour as sexual harassment: that it is unwanted by the recipient. In many other areas of life, if someone doesn't like something she or he says so. If someone steals your personal belongings, you don't usually remain silent about this treatment, but tell your friends, relatives, colleagues at work and maybe the police. If someone dents the door of a car when it is parked in a car park, the owner of the car doesn't keep quiet about the annoying dent in the paintwork but, again, tells people about her unlucky experience.

However, sexual harassment doesn't work in this way. Women who are harassed often feel it is their own fault, that they somehow asked for it and that the matter is too embarrassing to talk about. So while she may not like the way the harasser touches her, puts his arm on her shoulder, or leans over her when she is working at her desk, it doesn't mean that the woman feels she can say anything. Silence does not imply consent. It is more likely to mean that the recipient feels that she is not in a position to tell the harasser to stop, or to ask him not to repeat the behaviour.

This is why sexual harassment is much more significant for women than it is for men. Sexual harassment can only be effective if it employs the power differential in our society. Confronting a perpetrator of harassment is partly to do with your confidence and status, partly to do with your beliefs about personal rights, partly to do with how you think a request for particular behaviour to stop will be respected, partly to do with being able to label the behaviour as sexual harassment rather than merely classifying it as something you 'just don't like', and partly to do with your level of assertiveness. In any case, it should not be the employee's job to teach her boss how to behave. Suggesting that women must take responsibility for controlling their male colleagues reinforces the stereotype that women are the keepers of society's moral standards and codes of conduct.

Sexual harassment or sexual attention?

One of the problems with enabling, encouraging and relying on the recipient to name harassment arises from the fact that how each sex behaves has largely been laid down over many years: there is a vast panoply of attitudes to which men and women are expected to conform. There is nothing wrong with this in principle, but it can lead to problems in contemporary life, where work and leisure opportunities and patterns are new. Because, generally, women and girls are taught to be passive, sexually non-aggressive, caring, mindful of others' needs, and biddable, some women find it extremely difficult to name unwanted behaviour as sexual harassment, let alone do something about it. This problem is most evident with girls in schools, young women in universities and with first-time female employees, mainly young inexperienced women and girls.

Because of the mores and traditions regarding sexual encounters and roles in the dominant culture, women and girls are subject to requests for dates, comments from male strangers about their dress, hair and smiles, their legs, bodies and breasts. One consequence of the general expectation that females must wait to be invited or approached by a male who is interested in them is that they may welcome as attention behaviours which should more properly be called harassment.

The principles of sexual harassment

I would like now to return to the list of behaviours which I classified in the last chapter as consensual sexual behaviours. These were: wolf-whistles, pats, strokes, nudges, cuddles, winks, nods, kisses, repeated requests for dates, sexual innuendoes about clothes, body size, hair, leisure and weekend activities, presents, sexual jokes and *double entendres*. As I have said, these same behaviours may, under different circumstances, constitute sexual harassment. While it is difficult to be categorical about what behaviours are sexually harassing, there are some principles which are agreed upon by all those interested in finding a common language for countering particular unwanted sexual behaviour in the workplace.

- It is the perception of the recipient which determines whether behaviour is wanted or unwanted.

- Sexual harassment is to do with the abuse of power and nothing about wanting a sexual relationship.

- Sexual harassment is not mutual, genuine sexual attention.

- Sexual harassment is unwanted, unwelcome and unsolicited by the recipient.

- The intentions of the perpetrator should not be taken into account when determining a case of sexual harassment.

- Sexual harassment should be quantified in terms of frequency not in terms of severity.

- Every person has a different threshold of tolerance, making any one action sexual harassment or not sexual harassment depending on the recipient's perception.

- There is no definitive list of behaviours which constitute sexual harassment at all times and in all places.

- Sexual harassment is largely determined by the relationship or non-relationship between the two parties involved.

- There is no objective criterion for sexual harassment.

- The use of sexual harassment by perpetrators is to do with sexual politics and thus some recipients may not recognize it for what it is.

- Sexual harassment can be suffered by recipients both directly and indirectly.

Types of harassment

Whilst I have just argued that sexual harassment and mutual sexual behaviour may actually involve the same acts, it is important to look beyond these and search for clearer differences.

Behaviour which constitutes sexual harassment can be divided into three main categories, depending on how common it is, rather than how severe. Sexual harassment which is frequent and commonplace is that which is also usually irritating and banal, for which the perpetrator is unlikely to be disciplined, and is highly unlikely to have a case brought against him. The next category is that which is less frequent but of a kind where internal disciplinary proceedings may be put in place. The third category is fairly rare but constitutes criminal behaviour and can be brought to an Industrial Tribunal (see Chapter 13: Taking a Case to an Industrial Tribunal).

I will take each one separately. The first type of sexual harassment is irritating and low level. An analogy to this type of harassment would be having your car backed into whilst it was parked in a multi-storey car park, graffiti written on the wall of your house, or the plant containers outside your front door stolen. Even if the police caught the perpetrator, it is unlikely that they would be taken to court. The kinds of sexually harassing behaviours which are in the same category as these 'crimes' would be: wolf-whistles; pats, strokes, winks, sexist terms like 'love', 'dear', 'petal' and 'sweetheart', sexist jokes and patronizing behaviour.

The second category of behaviour constituting sexual harassment would probably be taken seriously by the organization in which the recipient works, but is unlikely to be taken into the public arena. I have known cases where women have been grabbed on the breasts, had hands thrust down their blouses or had their bottoms patted, or had been persistently asked for dates, or their sex lives questioned, but criminal proceeding were not invoked.

The third type is that which is unlawful behaviour. Into this category come five areas which can constitute criminal offences: assault (physical or sexual), indecent exposure (masturbation, nudity), molestation (groping, grabbing, kissing and fondling), obscene 'phone calls and nuisance letters, and threatening behaviour.

However, whether one complains to a responsible person within the organization or takes it up with a view to taking the case to an Industrial Tribunal will be determined to a large extent by the context in which the behaviour occurs. It will depend on the frequency of the act (once, twice, constantly); who did it, (a boss, a clerk, a colleague, a caretaker); how the recipient reacted (ignored it, became stressed, left the job), what the harassment involved, and if there were any witnesses or circumstantial evidence.

I list sample behaviours of each type below.

Type One

- leering, wolf-whistles, name-calling, winking, facial gestures, grunts and groans

- sexual/sexist jokes, comments or innuendoes

- sexually explicit page three pin-ups, calendar pin-ups

- requests for dates after being turned down

- sexist ridicule or trivialization of one's job performance by a colleague.

Type Two

- subtle or overt pressure for sexual activity

- uncalled-for physical contact, deliberate brushing past

- sexist ridicule or trivialization of one's job performance by one's boss

- invasive questions about one's private life

- obvious playing with own genitals.

Type Three

- assault (physical or sexual)

- indecent exposure (masturbation, nudity)

- molestation (groping, grabbing, kissing, and fondling)

- obscene 'phone calls and nuisance letters

- threatening behaviour.

What sexual harassment is not

Whilst it is important to know what sexual harassment is, it is also necessary to know what it isn't. We all know what we like and what we don't like, whom we have an affinity with and whom we don't. Often, however, the message doesn't come across to the other person - the potential lover or the potential harasser. It is important to recognize that about 45 per cent of workers meet their future partner in the workplace. One might well ask how these two people managed to weave their way through the treacherous sea of confusion between what is sexual harassment and what is sexual attraction!

Clearly, the first criterion we have for a wanted sexual relationship is that the two people concerned wish for the behaviour to happen. It is consensual. Two people engaged in setting up a sexual relationship use flirting, sexual innuendo, sexual nods, winks, waves, touches and comments to attract the other person's attention. They send each other notes, make excuses to ring each other up several times a day, give each other presents. And it is happening between both people; both people are doing the calling, the smiling, the winking, the chatting up, the laughing and the flirting. It may be sexist and sex-stereotyped, but it is by mutual consent.

Similarly, friendly repartee, jokes or pranks in which both or all parties join does not constitute harassment if there are only willing participants. It is not all right if one member of a group is cajoled into doing things against her will because the group won't listen.

Sexual harassment is also not specific social behaviour which has arisen as a result of a group working together over a period of time. If all the members of the group are consenting to this behaviour, it cannot be labelled as sexual harassment.

Thus a group who have worked, played, struggled and learned together over a period of time may be more 'friendly' towards one another than a different group of workers. A group identity may be born out of this unique team spirit and behaviours may occur which, in other circumstances, would be considered too risqué, too intimate, too personal and constituting sexual harassment. However, if freely entered into and enjoyed by each person in this group, it does not constitute sexual harassment. This does not imply, however, that it is not sexist: it might well be.

Of course, if a new person joining the group doesn't like this kind of treatment and makes a complaint, what was hitherto acceptable may suddenly become unacceptable and therefore have to stop.

Lastly, there is the case of consenting adults engaged in sexual relationships within the workplace. The two involved may be married to other people, they may be gay; they may, in another's view, be wrongly or badly suited by age, experience, education, religion or race, etc. People in an organization engaging in a sexual relationship which contravenes someone else's personal morals are not perpetrating sexual harassment. It only becomes such if the two people concerned begin behaving inappropriately in the workplace, by kissing and cuddling, touching or playing sexually, for example. Then, as an outsider and a third party witnessing this behaviour, if you feel embarrassed and are prevented from doing your job effectively as a result, you have a case for lodging a complaint.

Do women ask for it?

Let us now turn to another side of the argument. It is without doubt true that some women and girls engage in sex-stereotyped behaviour which leads some men to make sexual comments or touch them in ways which they believe are appropriate and in order. Coquetry, coyness, incompetence, frailty, nervousness, and inefficiency are ways in which some women gain sexual attention. These, as much as men's behaviour, are learned. Indeed, there are some women who would feel ignored and sexually 'unappreciated' if comments, gestures, strokes and pats were not forthcoming. The problem is that some women like unsolicited sexual attention, describing it as pleasurable and desirable, whereas other women find the same behaviour, by the same man, to be humiliating and embarrassing. So what can be done?

First, we have to be clear as to who decides what constitutes sexual harassment and what constitutes sexual attention. The person on the receiving end of the treatment must decide whether they like it or not. If she doesn't like it and wants it to stop, it's sexual harassment. That seems clear. But is it the case that if she doesn't mind it isn't sexual harassment? This is not so clear.

Another aspect of this question, though, is the issue of provocation. Consider the comments of a magistrate about a woman's clothes. He clearly thought that the incident had been caused as a result of how she was dressed and her flaunting demeanour and that she was therefore responsible for provoking the sexually harassing behaviour. (Please also note that he calls the young woman *girl*.) The magistrate is summing up for an Industrial Tribunal:

> The Industrial Tribunal were entitled to take into account the fact that on occasions the appellant wore clothes at work which were scanty and provocative, as an element in deciding whether the harassment to which she was subjected constitutes a detriment. If a girl on the shop floor goes around wearing provocative clothes and flaunting herself, it is not unlikely that other work people - particularly men - will make remarks about it. It is an inevitable part of life on the shop floor. If she then complains that she has suffered detriment, the tribunal is entitled to look at the circumstances. (Quoted in *Making Advances* BBC Training Videos, 1993, p.19).

This shows the confusion that still exists about this issue. To claim that men are provoked into sexually harassing women by the kind of clothes they wear is to misunderstand the basic point about sexual harassment: that the recipient's feelings are crucial.

Learning to put up with sexual harassment

In my work as a teacher, over many years I frequently came across cases of unsolicited sexual behaviour which female students accepted, or at least were resigned to, as part and parcel of their lives as girls in that school. Was the treatment they were receiving at the hands of the boys sexual harassment? If asked, they said they didn't mind it. But they said this even about outrageously humiliating behaviour like having Tampax taken from their school bag and thrown around the room, accompanied by loud jeers about blood and smell and eggs and mess. When asked, they also said they certainly didn't want anything said about the incident to the boys. Why?

I suppose one of the answers lies in their belief about themselves, their self-esteem, the roles they have learned to play about not being aggressive, passively accepting their lot, and perhaps even messages about having deserved this treatment. But they had not had access to consciousness raising-groups (see Chapter 1), they had not had information that led them to conclude that this behaviour was a manifestation of the roles that men and women are conditioned to playing: men having power and authority over women whether they like it or not.

Catherine Hall, whom I quoted in Chapter 1, has called this understanding of the power relations between men and women 'sexual politics'. The girls in school did not understand the power relations between the boys and girls in their class, at their school or in society generally at a political level; they had not had the opportunity or time to share their experiences, to name the behaviour and to find that it was commonplace amongst all the girls in that school. But they had learned that to get a boyfriend, to be seen to be part of the group, one did not publicly put down boys, complain about unwanted male behaviour, make the scene more unpleasant and embarrassing for the girls or the boys, or incite the wrath of one's peers.

What this means is that the criterion of 'unwanted attention' is not completely adequate. As an employer or manager, you may deem it to be in the best interests of your staff to stop a particular behaviour about which no complaint has been made. It will then of course be sensible to carry out a training programme.

Just because a woman has accepted certain behaviour for some years, putting up with sexist or sexual banter and put-downs, does not mean that she will not change her understanding and tolerance of such treatment through education. I have already talked about C-R groups and it is in environments of this kind that women and girls come to change their understanding of sexualized comments and behaviour.

Can men be part of the solution?

Of course men must be involved in countering sexual harassment at a number of levels. First, they must be made more aware of the treatment they are giving to whom and for what reason. Men must search their souls to find why they consider they have the right to pat, cuddle and stroke particular women, especially if they are their boss. Why do they consider it all right to make comments about a woman's body, her clothes, her hair, her smile or her eyes? Why do they ask personal questions about a woman's life?

Second, because there are more male managers than women managers, men have to take a lead in initiating training and education in the area of sexual harassment. They must release money to provide workshops for all people in the organization. They must support and be seen to support the training, perhaps opening the first session of each workshop to express their confidence in its value.

Third, they must take a lead in role modelling equity and non-discriminatory practice and show the workforce how employees are expected to behave towards each other in a professional way. If managers make sexist comments about people, tell sexist jokes, or make sexist assumptions about men and women's roles, this will create an ethos in which sexual harassment is seen to be acceptable.

Fourth, men managers can help women employees realise their own power and potential. They must encourage them to take responsibility for their own jobs and not rely on their male colleagues to do the bits of their work which the female worker considers not suited to a woman. I have described earlier how some women use behaviour which encourages sexist and discriminatory actions and comments. If a woman is being coy and not accepting her responsibilities in the workplace, it is important that managers, rather than patronizing her, should explain why this behaviour is unacceptable. This will encourage her to accept her workload and find strategies which will enable her to do her work without having to manipulate male colleagues.

CHAPTER THREE

Sexual Harassment: The Power Dimension

Introduction

One of the questions frequently raised is the extent to which men can be sexually harassed. The answer rests mostly on one's understanding of the power dimensions within society. It is my contention that, given the structures in our culture, sexual harassment is not an appropriate name to give to unwanted sexual attention that men occasionally receive from women; a better name for sexist banter, put-downs, or unwanted declarations of love by women of men is *sexist hassle*. Including this type of behaviour in the term 'sexual harassment' obscures a significant distinction which is an aid to understanding the phenomenon and finding defences against it. Of course, this is not to say that sexist hassle should be ignored. Any behaviour which demeans others needs to be stopped.

Can men be sexually harassed?

In this chapter I want to consider the structural forces that govern the ways in which sexual harassment (for women) is delivered, perceived and experienced with its consequent effects, and to distinguish this from the conditions under which men receive sex-based harassment, sexist hassle or unwanted sexual attention.

Consider for example a male university student who works in a canning factory during the summer vacation and during this period, on a daily basis, is picked on, humiliated, degraded and de-bagged by a group of women packers. The young man feels embarrassed, shocked, unable to tell the management, and longs for the vacation to end.

The question is, is this sexual harassment? If so why? And if not why not?

There is a series of questions one can ask concerning the outcome of this unwanted sexual treatment. I would argue that the consequences for this young man and his future life are very different from those found by women.

- Did the young man return home and decide not to go down to the pub for a drink because a group of women had looked at his 'privates' and had humiliated him?

- Would he generalize from these specific women and be afraid of all other women, saying he would rather stay in than go out in the dark to the local shop for fear of one of these women or one like her attacking him?

- Had only one of the women tried to de-bag him, would he have succumbed?

- Had he been 40 years old, would they have done it?

- Was this young man inured to treatment of this kind from the girls he went to school with, his women teachers, women bus drivers, barmaids and women who serve in shops?

- Was he so used to behaviour of this kind that it had become unremarkable and 'normal' female behaviour?

- Would this young man change his career path as a result of this three months' canning factory experience?

- Would he experience similar treatment right through his career, and sometimes be forced to leave his job as a result of this behaviour?

To each of these questions, I think, I would have to say 'No'. The point is that a man's experience of unwanted sexual attention has very different consequences to those suffered by women. For each of the questions above, the answer to the corresponding question for a woman would most probably have been 'Yes'.

The reason for the difference lies in the power dimension of an experience of sexual harassment for a woman; a dimension which is usually of little importance in a man's subjection to the same treatment.

Power

There are three kinds of power necessary to transform unwanted sexual attention into sexual harassment, respectively manifested individually, structurally and culturally.

Individual power

Individually, both men and women can give and receive sexual attention which is unwanted by the recipient. However, people who have enough individual power to cause their advances to be painful, silencing and unstoppable are much more likely to be male than female.

But why do men have more individual power than women? The greater proportion of people in our Western society who have status, position, educational opportunity, economic wealth, and inheritance are men. Because of what our society deems as important, these attributes provide access to power and privilege. It is usually men who make and implement laws and government policies, decide how money will be allocated, make judgements about defence, education, health and industry. An integral part of the educational process for boys during their school years is that they learn to expect certain rights, privileges and positions. Further, in the education system as it stands, it is boys mainly who acquire confidence and self-esteem, crucial to them when they take their places as leaders of the country.

A woman who is sexually harassed by a man with individual power does not have access to equal rights. Women who complain about the treatment they are receiving are often called 'hysterics', 'trouble-makers' or 'liars'. Moreover, they are less able to defend themselves physically, are less likely to be supported by the employer, have fewer resources to pay a professional to fight their case, and are more wary about complaining. The result is that women remain silent and men continue harassing.

Structural power

Sexual harassment, however, is not based on individual power alone. The congregation of men in positions of power creates structural power, the second of the sources of power needed for sexual harassment to be effective.

For unwanted sexual attention or sexist hassle to become sexual harassment, perpetrators must be able to make use of sources of power which nurture behaviour of this kind, and must know that their own perception of what they have done will be acceptable to most people. Perpetrators have access to a power base which can provide this support, located within the structures of our society: the organizations in which they work are patriarchal and this affects the mores and conventions generally.

On this power base it is possible to silence recipients, to convince victims that it is better to resign a job than fight a case, to confuse recipients so that they think they are responsible for the harassment, to threaten recipients with the sack if they pursue a case, to mislead claimants into thinking they will not be believed if they make a complaint, to disempower recipients so that they feel unable to fight back and tell the perpetrator to stop and go away and, lastly, the biggest duplicity of all, to make this unwanted treatment so unremarkable that it is seen as 'normal' behaviour by most and unacceptable by so few.

Organizations have the ability to make sexual harassment almost invisible to the human eye, and if not invisible, then at least 'normal'; they can make the impact of sexual harassment negligible by ignoring the consequences both for the victim and for the organization itself; they can make it difficult, if not impossible, to prove that sexual harassment happened. The structures of law and the understanding of truth are patriarchal and institutionalized. Men have almost exclusive access to this kind of structural power.

Corroborative evidence is usually needed to prove a case. Much highly distressing sexual harassment happens privately between the two parties concerned. There are no witnesses. It will be the recipient's word against the perpetrator's: his position against hers; his worth, salary, reputation, wife and family stacked against a complaint by a dispensable, low-waged, 'hysterical' woman 'out for revenge' or with an 'over-active imagination'.

Within the structure of society there is an implicit ethos, a way of working or behaving usually unchallenged and all-pervasive. Organizations have budgets for the use of particular projects, rooms for use by particular groups, timetables for observance by all employees, soft and comfortable chairs, hard and wooden chairs, large carpeted offices with isolated expansive desks, and small vinyl floored offices with a quantity of desks. Some people have individual personal computers, others share them between groups. Many women do not have expensively decorated offices, access to training budgets, or the authority to change policies.

Within organizations there are accepted ways of behaving. In one that I heard of, there was a snooker table in the staffroom, where the men played billiards each lunch time. The women were pushed, literally, to the edges of the room while the men played. In some organizations there are even areas in which naked or semi-naked pin-ups of women's bodies are displayed.

Why are there so few effective policies, so few sexual harassment officers in each organization, so little money for training and development, and so little government intervention and support for the elimination of sexual harassment in offices and factories? Organizations which have men at the helm largely ignore the cries from women for action.

Incidentally, if sexual harassment were a problem for men, it is likely that the laws would have been strengthened, the penalties for not having effective policies would be severe, and training would be government sponsored, monitored and evaluated. Whilst it is claimed that statistics show that sexual harassment is a problem for large numbers of women in organizations, especially organizations which are predominantly male-oriented, only 40 per cent of workplaces have policies on sexual harassment. One hundred percent of workplaces have policies on Health and Safety. The Sex Discrimination Act (1975) has been in operation for 18 years, yet there is no explicit reference to sexual harassment within this Act. (Since 1987, however, sexual harassment has been seen as unlawful behaviour which contravenes the Sex Discrimination Act.)

Sexual harassment thrives while organizations maintain that it doesn't exist or is not a problem, and sexism, sex discrimination and sexist behaviours are denied as being anything other than the normal behaviour of men.

Cultural power

The third form of power which underpins the continuation of sexual harassment is provided by the cultural bases on which traditions and mores are built. *Boys will be boys* is a common enough saying, reflecting an indulgent attitude to the misdemeanours of men in the workplace. As I have already argued, generally women and girls are regarded as sexual prey, and men as sexual predators.

Whilst some traditions and mores have changed, the customary way in which girls and boys, men and women, begin sexual relations is age-old.   Men ask women out. Women stay silent and passive, giving out particular signs and signals, waiting for the 'phone to ring and a date to be forthcoming. A woman is collected from her home by the boyfriend/man-friend/male lover in his car. Although today the man may not pay all the evening's expenses, he will pay the larger share, partly because it is likely that he is earning more and, anyway, that is how things are supposed to be. (Waiters still give the restaurant bill to the man at the table even if the table has been booked in the name of the woman.) It will be the man who leads sexually, deciding when, where, the frequency and the duration. Sexual harassment is closely connected to this gender division. Whilst women are seen as possessions, as objects, as things to be touched, played with, patted, commented on, as second-class workers, as dispensable colleagues, sexual harassment will continue.

Returning to the question: can men be sexually harassed?

Perhaps at this point it would be helpful to return to the student in the canning factory and to see whether, given these three kinds of power, the treatment he received was sexual harassment.

First, the individual power. Certainly it is true that the women in the factory had power over the student and they used and abused it. But this is probably the only place that they had some power, and it wasn't very much. For the period of time the student was working there, in sexually hassling him they had wrested some power and had enjoyed it. In the pub, in the street, in the union, through the media, in books, on the bus, in their home and in every other sphere these women had less power and authority than their male counterparts. Outside this factory they had no power over this male student.

Furthermore, the type of behaviour experienced by the young man is unusual. It is not a common experience for a man to be ridiculed, demeaned and de-bagged. No doubt it would have come as a shock to him, because he was not used to being touched and seen merely as a sexual object. The way in which the factory women behaved is not a typical experience for most men, and I would suggest that one of the reasons he would have remained silent was not because he feared the managers would not believe him, or he thought he would get the sack, or he was afraid they would accuse him of provoking the women, or he believed they would see him as a trouble-maker. He remained quiet because he was ashamed that the manager would laugh, think him unmanly and a wimp to have let women take advantage of him.

The second form of power, structural power, was also not a weapon on which the women could rely. I have already described how unusual it is for women to behave like this, and how they had wrested a piece of power for themselves. This form of behaviour is not condoned by society, is not described as normal behaviour for women to perpetrate on men. It is not supported by other more public displays of sexist material such as page three men, male calendars, hoardings with semi-naked men advertizing life assurance, male pin-ups, sexual jokes and innuendoes about men or male behaviour which dominate the rest of society. So for this male student the sexist hassle was a unique experience that would be condemned by society and which he is unlikely to undergo once he has left this factory.

Lastly, cultural power is also denied women. It is not seen as part of women's behaviour to sexually pursue, to set the pace in a sexual relationship, to pat, touch and make remarks about what men look like. Equally, women are not expected to be sexually aggressive, although this example shows they can be. Such behaviour would not be condoned as 'women being women' or as an oestrogen surge which renders women incapable of sexual control.

So one's ability to sexually harass, as opposed to sexually hassle, is built upon one's access to these three forms of power. Male individuals can choose whether to use their personal power to sexually harass or not. Their behaviour is tacitly supported within the structures of the organizations as well as the wider governmental, legal and educational establishments. And finally, the male colleagues of those men who do sexually harass a female colleague will most probably murmur things like, 'He's a bit of a lad', 'Good on him', 'Well, she's been asking for it', and so on.

Women just do not have access to these three power bases. This leads me to conclude that sexual harassment is uniquely a woman's problem. The effect of sexual harassment is to confine and limit girls' and women's capacity to operate in the public sphere. The motivation for sexual harassment is firmly located in power and the maintenance of that power.

CHAPTER FOUR

Statistics

Introduction

The extent to which sexual harassment is a problem has been quantified by a number of organizations using a variety of questionnaires, 'phone-ins and other such means. Little qualitative research has been done, however. This is partly due to the fact that this research method is invariably more time-consuming than others, because it involves in-depth conversations with people over a period of time, is often dependent on a rapport being built up between the researcher and the research participant so that issues below the surface can be discussed and unravelled, and it requires the research participant to consider her or his response in depth and to have time to think over possible answers, and to ask questions, to clarify certain points and to understand in detail what it is the researcher is getting at.

Questionnaires and research methods

The results quoted below have all been obtained from quantitative research. This is the method where a questionnaire is sent out to a number of people at random and they are asked to fill it in and return it. People who are interested in sexual harassment will return the questionnaire, others who are not so interested will probably not reply. The results are therefore biased and it is difficult to make decisions about what to do about sexual harassment in the workplace on such inconsistent figures.

Most surveys are done on the basis of asking questions of people who do not have access to the question setter to check what is meant, to ask what to do if the answers they have don't fit the question or the space, if they want to put in additional things to explain certain points or the question is ambiguous. Some questionnaires rely on the respondent having a clear understanding of the subject in hand. This may be a sensible way of collecting information if we are interested in the likes and dislikes of supermarket products but is hardly adequate for finding out information about sensitive issues like sexual harassment.

A very obvious problem is that of definition of the term itself, to cover the whole range of behaviours, feelings, attitudes and values.

In a survey conducted on 19th October 1991, by NOP for *The Independent on Sunday*, it was found that only 16 per cent of women considered that they had been subjected to sexual harassment at work If we look at the responses it becomes clear that there is a wide discrepancy in what people see as constituting sexual harassment.

The following behaviours were classed by the given percentage of women as NOT being sexual harassment.

Having one's appearance commented on by a male boss	57%
Being called darling	59%
Constantly being asked for a date by the same person	12%
Being touched by a supervisor	8%
Being invited by the boss to watch porn films with him	2%

Women who are politically aware would claim that sexual harassment at work includes looks, wolf-whistles, pin-ups, sexist comments and assumptions, patronizing words like 'dear' and 'love', as well as unwanted touching and patting.

Other research on the prevalence of sexual harassment has come up with the following percentages of people who claim they have been subjected to such behaviour.

1981	Cooper and Davidson	52%
1982	Alfred Marks Bureau	51%
1983	Civil and Public Services Association	30%
1983	Leeds Trade Union & Community Resource and Information Centre	59%
1987	Labour Research Department	73%
1987	National Union of Teachers	72%
1989	Marplan	61%
1989	Suzy Lamplugh Trust	13.5%
1991	Police Department (Anderson *et al.*, 1993)	53%
1993	Mori Poll for the BBC	30%
1993	Industrial Society	54%

These studies may represent the 'tip of the iceberg' as many respondents only identify blatant and overt behaviour as constituting sexual harassment. Many respondents only mention physical harassment rather than verbal and non-verbal behaviour, graffiti, looks and gestures as constituting sexual harassment.

Sexual harassment cases

In the five years after the Jean Porcelli Case, Industrial Tribunals decided 97 sexual harassment cases,[1] 53 of which were successful. The cases were compared to see whether the type of person representing the recipient had any bearing on the outcome.

---

* Figures taken from *The New Law Journal*, November 8th 1991, p.1514.

Representative	Total	Successful	Percentage
Barrister	15	12	80%
Solicitor	39	20	51%
Law Centre	2	0	0
CAB	12	6	50%
Trade Union	3	3	100%
Self	7	4	57%
Other	10	2	25%
Not stated	9	6	66%

The New Law Journal states that these figures are unusual for two reasons. First, the 55 per cent success rate of sexual harassment cases is quite high compared to other types of discrimination cases such as discrimination in recruitment, promotion, dismissal, etc., brought under the Sex Discrimination Act. In other sex discrimination cases only some 30 per cent of cases heard at a tribunal are successful. Second, the proportion of applicants who had legally qualified representatives (56 per cent) is unusually high: in tribunal cases generally only about one-third of applicants have legal representation. It can therefore be argued that one of the reasons that the success rate is high is that those bringing cases of sexual harassment decide to use professional representation. Where the applicant represented themselves, only 20 per cent were successful. In cases where legal representation was sought, nearly 60 per cent won their case. The high success rate may also indicate that tribunals are particularly sympathetic to this type of complaint, which so often involves quite offensive behaviour by an employer or manager towards an employee.

The role of women in society

Below is some interesting information about the role of women in society: quotes from eminent men about their role; employment areas occupied by men and women; dates in some countries when women were first allowed to vote; and some statistics of university entrance for men and women.

> Women constitute half the world's population, perform nearly two-thirds of its work hours, receive one-tenth of the world's income and own less than one-hundredth of the world's property. (United Nations Report, 1980).

> A judge said of women and girls: 'Human experience in the court has shown that women and girls, for all sorts of reasons and sometimes for no reason at all, tell a false story which is extremely easy to fabricate but extremely difficult to refute'. (Lowe, in Hopkins, 1984, p.81).

> [Jean-Jacques Rousseau, an educationalist of the eighteenth century, writing about girls of that period said:] a 'woman's education must ... be planned in relation to men. To be pleasing in his sight, to win his respect and love, to train him in childhood, to tend to him in his manhood, to counsel and console, to make his life pleasant and happy, these are the duties of women for all times, and this is what she should be taught when she is young'. (J-J Rousseau, 1762, Ch.1).

> [William Acton, (1813-75), a British expert on sex issues writing in the nineteenth century, claimed that if a woman refused her husband sexual relations over a period of time this would be highly detrimental to his health, particularly if he happened to be strongly sexually disposed. He continued:] 'The more conscientious the husband and the stronger his sexual feelings, the more distressing are the sufferings he is doomed to undergo, ultimately too often ending in impotence.' (Hellerstein et al., 1981, p.179).

Women and politics

Women and the vote

Dates when women were first entitled to vote in:			
New Zealand	1893	Finland	1906
Norway	1913	Poland	1918
Sweden	1919	Netherlands	1919
Germany	1919	USA	1920
UK	1928	Brazil	1932
Turkey	1934	France	1944
Belgium	1948	Greece	1952
Switzerland	1971	Liechtenstein	1984

Women entering cabinet positions

Dates when women were first appointed to cabinet in:			
Poland	1918	Finland	1926
UK	1929	USA	1933
Norway	1945	Sweden	1947
France	1947	New Zealand	1947
Greece	1956	Netherlands	1956
West Germany	1961	Belgium	1965
Switzerland	1971	Turkey	1971
Brazil	1982	Liechtenstein	1984

Women's and men's employment trends

- 94% of secretaries are women

- 85% of managing directors are men

- 4% of High Court judges are women

- 95% of surgeons are men

- 14% of parliamentarians are women

- 49% of teachers in secondary schools are women

- 85% of headteachers in secondary schools are men

- 82% of shop assistants are women

- 95% of bank managers are men

- 91% of office cleaners are women

- 87% of nurses are women

- 97% of hand machinists in the textile industry are women

- 3% of chief executives are women

*University undergraduate entries (domicile UK) in thousands:**

Subject	Women	Men
Language-related	20.0	8.5
Social Sciences	16.4	17.9
Medicine/Dentistry	10.0	11.5
Biological Sciences	9.9	7.8
Humanities	7.5	8.3
Physical Sciences	5.7	15.1
Studies allied to Medicine	4.6	2.3
Mathematical Sciences	3.9	12.0
Business/Financial studies	4.0	6.2
Engineering/Technology	3.6	25.1
Vet. Science & Agric./related studies	2.0	2.2
Creative Arts	2.6	1.6
Education	2.8	0.7
Architecture & related studies	1.1	2.5
Library & Information Science	0.1	0.1
All Subjects	110.0	138.0

---

* University Statistics (1989/90) Vol. 1, *Staff and Students*, DES.

CHAPTER FIVE

Consequences and Legal Implications

Introduction

Sexual harassment is a phenomenon which has numerous, varied and severe consequences. It has a direct effect on the recipient of course, but also it concerns others. These include the harasser himself, other workers who know it is happening and perhaps are worried that it might happen to them too, and the recipient's friends, family and relatives. It affects productivity and workplace morale, and a mishandled case of harassment can involve time-consuming meetings with managers, directors and witnesses, report writing, disruption of the workforce, solicitor's fees and the time and costs involved in defending a case at an Industrial Tribunal. I will consider each of these areas separately.

The recipient

A case of harassment can have an enormous effect on a recipient. Sexual harassment hits right at the heart of a person's confidence and self-esteem, eating away at their ability to do their job, their friendships with work colleagues and their private relationships.

In the short term the recipient may not only suffer from depression, headaches, stomach disorders, and other stress-related illnesses, but the harassment may destroy her self-confidence, her trust in people and her ability to do her job. As a result she may well take time off, begin to come into work late, leave early and have extended lunch hours. Under the kind of stress brought on by sexual harassment the recipient may become tearful, nervous, short-tempered and erratic in her behaviour. If her job entails working with machinery the vexation may result in her temporary loss of concentration causing injury to herself and other workers/people.

Her family life may suffer as she becomes moody, withdrawn, aggressive and difficult to live with. In order to hide and forget the abuse she may turn to nicotine, alcohol or drugs to ease the pain.

In the long term, if the harassment continues, she may cause an accident, injure herself or leave her job or place of study. If she leaves her studying and 'drops out', she may be disqualified, due to lack of exam results, from taking up her chosen career, thus the harassment having financial and life quality consequences too. If she resigns her job she may find it difficult to find another job on a similar pay scale and terms. In the final event, a sexually harassed person may commit suicide.

The perpetrator

A perpetrator of harassment will also suffer in various ways although probably not as far-reaching as those of his recipient. He will probably not be as efficient at his work if he watches for opportunities to follow, touch and harass colleagues. His mind will not be solely on his job, he may be easily distracted, possibly causing severe damage to himself or others. In addition, colleagues of both sexes, disapproving of how he treats certain individuals may avoid working with him and keep away. This may result in him being unable to work effectively in a team situation.

The organization

It is not just the individuals who suffer from sexual harassment. The institution in which the harassment happens cannot function as well as it could if employees are engaged in sexually harassing behaviour.

One of the first things that will affect the institution is employee morale. Sexual harassment affects the whole working ethos, not just the harasser and the recipient. Other employees will lose faith in the organization's ability to lead, to manage and to stop unwanted behaviour such as this.

Dispirited employees cause lower productivity and thus a loss of earnings for the business. Staff absenteeism will increase, followed by greater staff turnover. Not only do the recipients of harassment leave, but so do others who find the working conditions impossible when incidents of sexual harassment are ignored or are dealt with ineptly.

Staff handing in their notice will result in the company having to advertize, recruit, re-train and allow for a period of settling in for the new employee, who, if the harasser hasn't been located and disciplined, or his behaviour changed, may end up by resigning herself a few months later.

Through sexual harassment a company may lose talented and valued employees. If staff hand in their notice after only a short period of time working, the business will have lost money on the training and professional development invested in that person. Also, attracting responsible and professional employees to an organization sometimes relies on public information about the way in which staff are treated. Bad publicity or rumours that sexual harassment is a problem which is not being dealt with will result in fewer top quality personnel applying for careers within that company.

Generally in a workplace in which sexual harassment occurs people are not performing to capacity and are distracted and made anxious by potential incidents. I have already warned of the danger of injury to individuals, but for the company this could mean higher compensation claims. For a company the effects of unresolved sexual harassment cases can also affect the willingness of employees to work overtime, work away from home, work at weekends and at other times where only a few personnel are in operation.

Legal implications

Employers have a responsibility to provide a sex discrimination-free work environment (see Chapter 11: The Role of Management). The Sex Discrimination Act, 1975, states that it is unlawful for an employer to treat a woman [or man] less favourably than the employer would treat a man [or woman]. This clause is extended to cover all employees from suffering sexual harassment at the hands of a colleague, boss or subordinate, whether or not the employer knew it was happening. It is both the harasser and the employer who are liable for the unlawful act.

An example of sexual harassment which could amount to a case of sex discrimination is where an employee makes sexist comments or touches a woman employee on her breasts or bottom. It is discrimination, because he would not treat a man in the same way. So a case of sexual harassment constituting sex discrimination rests on the kind of behaviour or treatment a person is given. (There needs to be some consideration of homosexuality, although there are no laws protecting men from sexual harassment by another man [or men] or of a woman [or women] sexually harassing another woman [or women].

There have been a number of Industrial Tribunal cases in which women have claimed that the treatment they received from a colleague constituted sexual harassment. Their cases have been upheld (see Chapter 4: Statistics).

One such case, and the first in which sexual harassment constituted sex discrimination, was that of Jean Porcelli. Mrs Porcelli was a school lab technician. Two male colleagues made lewd and sexually suggestive remarks to Mrs Porcelli and often took the opportunity to brush up against her in order to pass, even though there was ample room to move by without touching. They discussed pictures of naked women, comparing them with Jean and discussed pornographic videos in her presence.

In summing up the case, Lord Emslie stated: 'it was a particular kind of weapon based upon the sex of the victim, which ... would not have been used against an equally disliked man' (1986, Industrial Relations Law Report 134).

Here are more cases where a woman has successfully argued that it was because she was a woman that she suffered detriment. Mrs F alleged that her senior officer, Mr A, had persistently made sexual advances to her and was often aggressive and critical of her work. The Industrial Tribunal accepted Mrs F's evidence and held that Mr A's unwelcome advances constituted sex discrimination. They said that whilst Mr A could also be aggressive towards men, the aggression in this case was connected to the rejected advances and so were part and parcel of the sex discrimination (IDS Brief 362, December 1987).

Another case which clearly shows how detriment works is that of Ms W. Ms W was molested at an office party by a male friend of the company's managing director. Ms W eventually retaliated by tipping a glass of lager over him. She reported the incident to the director but the matter was not taken seriously and nothing was done. Three days later Ms W was dismissed without any real explanation.

The Industrial Tribunal held that Ms W had been unlawfully discriminated against. It was argued that it was unlikely that a male employee would have been harassed in the same way and it was improbable that he would have been sacked for resisting such advances.

Therefore sex discrimination or the sexual harassment of a woman [or man] is unlawful if it constitutes a detriment to her [or him].

Financial consequences

Apart from the human, legal and institutional consequences there are of course financial consequences to consider too.

Let's take a scenario, such as the one in which Mrs F claimed that Mr A had persistently made sexual advances to her and was often aggressive and critical of her work. I do not have any more details of the case than this, but I can hypothesize as to what was involved.

Let us assume that Mr A's sexual advances had been going on for six months He is a senior officer. If he spent between ten and fifteen minutes each day trying to chat up Mrs F, trying to touch her, making sexual innuendoes and the like, he would have wasted 60 minutes, or one hour a week. Over a period of six months this means 26 hours, over a year, 52 hours (or let's say a week's work).

If Mr A is earning £30,000 per annum he has wasted the company £576 for the week lost in sexually harassing Mrs F.

If we now look at Mrs F, the consequences are probably more devastating financially. During the first onslaught of sexual harassment, Mrs F finds that she cannot concentrate on her day-to-day tasks. In month one she wastes about 30 minutes a day trying to avoid Mr A's advances and thinking up ways of telling him to stop. She begins to get worried. After the first month the time that she is unable to work effectively rises to two hours per day, and the rest of the time she is not working to full capacity or with full concentration. (Month One: 40 hours @ £10 per hour = £400.)

In month two she is wasting up to three hours a day in avoidance strategies, hiding in the cloakrooms, repeating work that has mistakes, and talking to some of the other women about what is happening to her. She makes a number of mistakes that the company has to rectify, including forgetting to enter the times of important meetings with clients in the diary and she fails to turn up for some meetings herself. (Month Two: 60 hours @ £10 per hour = £600.)

In month three she begins to take time off work, at first only a day a week, although the harassment continues. (Month Three: 65 hours @ £10 per hour = £650.)

By month four she has to have a whole week off for stress. Her job is beginning to suffer seriously. Her colleagues are getting irritated by her lack of concentration. She is failing to meet deadlines and those people waiting for her are also held up. (Month Four: 85 hours @ £10 per hour = £850.)

In month five she loses a large order for the company because she forgot to send the potential client some essential information they required. (Month Five: order loss worth £5,000 plus another £850 in loss of time worked.)

In month six Mrs F is beginning to turn up for work late, is unable to concentrate at all and is depressed and stressed. Her colleagues have isolated her and are refusing to work with her. (Month Six: loss of work, plus absenteeism results in a loss of £1,000 in month six.)

The money that has been lost by Mrs F as a result of the sexual harassment in only six months has amounted to £9,250.

The personnel manager, Ms P is finally brought in to the case because one of Mrs F's colleagues goes and talks to her. Ms P spends five hours dealing with the initial informal discussions, exploring possible action plans and consulting with other managers in the organization.

Ms P feels that she doesn't know enough about sexual harassment so she rings a friend in another organization and spends about 40 minutes on the 'phone to her. The friend suggests she rings the union representative and this takes another 30 minutes. During the morning she tries to read an article about what to do about a case of sexual harassment and constructive dismissal.

After the personnel manager has spoken with Mrs F, Mrs F lodges a formal complaint with the Industrial Tribunal against both the company and Mr A.

Ms P spends 60 hours talking with the Advisory Conciliation and Advisory Service (ACAS), talking with Mrs F, preparing notes, collating information, discussing progress with the Managing Director and briefing solicitors. Her time is worth £20 per hour = £1,200.

Other employees need to take time off work to be interviewed by Ms P. They also spend some considerable time discussing the incident amongst themselves, watching the proceedings and the comings and goings from Ms P's office. Work suffers due to poor concentration: lost productivity approximately £1,000.

The solicitors' fees are £5,000.

Legal compensation is £8,000.

Advertising, recruiting and induction process for replacement for Mrs F costs £ 2,000

Ancillary costs - stationery, telephone calls, photocopying: £100.

The total cost of this case of sexual harassment has cost the organization somewhere in the region of £27,000.

Further costs could be taken into consideration too: i.e. loss of customers; loss of image; and personnel not wanting to work in that organization.

Putting in place a policy on sexual harassment and undertaking sexual harassment training throughout the organization would cost nothing like £27,000.

Consequences for family, friends and relatives of the recipient

The consequences for the recipient's family must not be ignored. When a member of a family is severely depressed, family and friends suffer too. For some, the stress on the family is too much and the family splits apart. Because the recipient is often ashamed of what is happening at work, fears that her husband/partner may blame her for encouraging it, thinks she will not be believed, or she should be handling it herself more effectively, she does not confide in her husband. This can cause problems. Equally some men are unable to handle their wife's sexual harassment and do believe the woman to be responsible; that she must have done something to encourage it; that she is being unfaithful, and they lose their trust. They may also get violent and want to attack the perpetrator.

CHAPTER SIX

Writing and Implementing a Sexual Harassment Policy

Introduction

In Chapter 3 of this book I have argued that sexual harassment is dependent on three forms of power; individual, structural and cultural. It has been explained how each form of power operates and the way in which these power forms serve as a backdrop for sexism, sexist behaviour, sexual discrimination and sexual harassment.

In order that sexual harassment be countered it is important to challenge behaviour which constitutes sexual discrimination. Within an organization this can be done by undermining two of the power bases – individual power and structural power – through policy writing and training. The most effective way of dealing with sexual harassment in an institution, on a long-term comprehensive level, is to devise and implement a sexual harassment policy, provide training for all personnel and ensure that the policy is monitored.

Writing a policy on sexual harassment

It is vitally important for an organization to have a policy on sexual harassment if there is a genuine commitment to stop sexually harassing behaviour. As many workers as possible should be consulted during the writing of such a policy, in order that a sense of involvement be engendered. If only a few people produce it the policy will be regarded as a document which management has foist on an unwelcoming workforce.

49

Awareness raising

However, consultation must be preceded by general awareness raising which could include:

- Informal meetings which address the issue. These do not necessarily have to be chaired by any one person, but a group of people could decide to hold a number of rolling meetings over a period of three months. They could arrange to meet various sections of the workforce to ask questions and have questions asked of them. For example:

  - Do you know what sexual harassment is?

  - Are you aware that sexual harassment may be unlawful if it constitutes sexual discrimination?

  - How should this organization help people become aware of this issue?

  - What do you think people who are harassed should do?

  - What would you like to do if you were harassed?

  - How should people respond who see others being sexually harassed?

  - Why do recipients of harassment remain silent about incidents?

  - Who are likely victims of unwanted sexual attention? What strategies could be used to protect them?

  - What role should the union play in policy formulation?

  - What is the role of the sexual harassment adviser? How should she or he be chosen?

  - What outside agencies are there to help?

- Short and easily read pamphlets produced to describe what sexual harassment is. These could be given to each employee with their pay packets.

- Questionnaires asking people to respond anonymously about incidents they have found uncomfortable, embarrassing or demeaning, or to identify areas of the organization which are potential or actual harassment sites.

- Questions asked of people leaving the organization pertaining specifically to whether they are leaving as a result of sexual harassment, or if they have ever experienced sexual harassment in the organization.

- The involvement of union representatives.

- Posters around the organization depicting a scene of unwanted sexual behaviour with information about where to go for help.

- A helpline.

Who should be involved?

The process of consultation is fundamental to the production of a workable, understandable and usable policy on sexual harassment, because the employees will then be more likely to feel responsible for and sympathetic to it. Inviting people to contribute can help ensure that it is a whole-institution document, not the property of one person, and that each employee will feel responsible for its implementation.

If sexual harassment is to be stopped systematically, all employees will need to have an understanding of what sexual harassment is and what the organization intends to do with employees who complain and with the perpetrators of sexual harassment. For it to be acknowledged as an important issue the managing director, the chair of the board, the chief executives and all other senior personnel should be involved from the very beginning. Without backing and support from the top, implementing a successful policy will be difficult.

What should the policy say?

The policy statement must clearly and simply state that all workers within the organization have a right to be treated with dignity; that sexual harassment in the workplace will be taken seriously and that something will be done about a complaint made; that sexual harassment denies the rights of the individual; that it can be prevented, or its prevalence or effect reduced, by empowering recipients to oppose it. The policy must also state that victimization will not be ignored and those found to be victimizing people who make complaints or who give evidence will be dealt with severely. Victimization is unlawful under the Sex Discrimination Act 1975 (see Chapter 11: The Role of Management). A policy on sexual harassment could include the following sections:

- A clear and explicit description of what constitutes sexual harassment. (Consideration must be given to verbal, non-verbal and physical harassment, graffiti, sexually explicit material, flashing and other manifestations of unwanted sexual attention.)

- An explicit grievance procedure, describing the steps a recipient must take when reporting a case of harassment (see Chapter 7: A Grievance Procedure.)

- What training methods are to be used to ensure all current staff, all new staff and all visiting or temporary consultants/workers understand the policy?

- How incidents of sexually harassing behaviour are to be recorded and monitored.

- How confidentiality is to be respected.

- A list of trained personnel to whom recipients can go when they wish to make a formal/informal complaint.

- A list of people outside the organization who may be able to provide help and advice on an incident of sexual harassment. These could include unions, Citizens Advice Bureaux, Industrial Tribunals, etc.

- Details of how post-harassment support will be provided to both recipient and harasser. It will be important to stress the underlying rationale that education is preferable to punishment.

- Details of how the efficacy of the policy and the education/training programmes will be evaluated.

The sexual harassment policy should state that prompt action will be taken as soon as an incident is notified. The action can take various forms, depending on the situation itself and the specific complaint. There can be no one way of dealing with cases, for all will be different. Thus, when dealing with an incident consideration must be given to:

- the frequency of the harassment

- the relationship of the recipient to the harasser

- the status of the recipient and the status of the harasser

- the nature of the behaviour

- the place/time of the harassment

- the wishes of the complainant*

- details of the Sex Discrimination Act (1975) need to be given, providing information to individuals about their rights under the law.

Possible setbacks in policy development

Sexual harassment is an emotive issue and it is unlikely that the passage of developing, writing and implementing the policy will be without incident. The major problem will probably be criticism by people who do not see that this is an important or worthwhile initiative (see Chapter 8: Countering the Sceptics, and Chapter 9: Countering Myths and Misconceptions). Their feelings about the proposed policy,

---

*In most cases the decision as to how an incident of sexual harassment will be dealt with will be up to the recipient, unless it is deemed that the behaviour is of such severity that action has to be taken irrespective of their wishes.

possibly directed at the instigators, may be expressed in a variety of ways:

- teasing

- trivialization of the issues/dismissive comments/jokes

- anger or hostility

- silence

- absence

- pedantic or petty criticisms of policy drafts.

Those who are likely to bear the brunt of this behaviour are female staff and people working towards producing the policy. It is important that this be considered within the organization and ways of supporting those people decided upon. Of course, it is ironic that some of the behaviour demonstrated throughout the policy development may well constitute sexual harassment. Also, in my experience, it is often those people who feel least confident about their attitudes and values who argue the fiercest and it is they who most need a 'softly softly' approach.

Now that it's written

Once the policy is written, it does not mean that everything can be forgotten. In order that the policy is seen to be a worthwhile, relevant document and one which is to be taken seriously, a number of strategies need to be employed.

- All personnel, including full-time and part-time staff, clients, customers, board members and students on work experience, should have access to a copy of the sexual harassment policy. Newcomers will also need to read and understand the policy when they arrive.

- Training should be part of the organization's annual programme.

- Sexual harassment should be addressed as a question in appraisal.

- Incidents of sexual harassment should be dealt with immediately, whenever and wherever they happen in the organization.

- The document should be updated and modified as relevant.

Policy writing and the EC

The EC suggests that a number of operations are necessary to eliminate sexual harassment from the workplace or to provide adequate training so that at the very least employees are aware of the issues and of the possible consequences if they fail to adhere to the staff policy. The European Council recommends that there be:

- formulation of a formal policy statement

- effective communication of the policy to all employees

- management responsibility for implementation of the policy

- training for managers, supervisors and any other officers given specific responsibilities for procedures.

- information on the company's harassment policy and procedures be included in induction and other training programmes.

CHAPTER SEVEN

A Grievance Procedure

Introduction

In this chapter I am going to describe a grievance procedure which moves from informal resolution, involving the face-to-face or one-to-one confrontation between the harasser and harassee, to a formal resolution possibly involving an Industrial Tribunal or other legal assistance. Of course whether any case is dealt with informally or formally will be dependent on the nature of the case, the frequency of the behaviour, the wishes of the recipient, the status of the perpetrator, the attitude of the harasser when confronted, the number of witnesses or other evidence, the duration of the harassment and many other factors.

It must be noted that this grievance procedure will only form a part of the process for resolving cases. It is recommended that each organization takes the principles described here and fits them into their own discipline procedures and regards cases of sexual harassment as cases of *misconduct*. Sexual harassment then becomes a disciplinary matter. Once this has been established it will be important for any verbal or written warnings given to a person regarding his sexually harassing behaviour to constitute part of the discipline procedure. Thus, only if a series of written or verbal warnings have been issued can any person be dismissed for sexual harassment, unless there is an incident of gross misconduct, or a criminal offence has been committed.

Complaints procedures

When a case of sexual harassment occurs, a recipient must be encouraged to seek out a named sexual harassment adviser in their organization, (see Chapter 10: Your Role as an Adviser) to discuss the path to take. The harasser might not be an employee of the organization; for example, he could be a workman on contract, a salesman from another company or a visitor. If the harasser is not within the recipient's organization, it would be more appropriate for the recipient to talk with the personnel manager or the managing director, who could take the matter up with the harasser's employer.

During the informal talk with the adviser, the recipient is encouraged to describe what happened, say who the perpetrator was, what effect his behaviour had, if there were any witnesses, what the recipient did about it, how it affected her, how often it happened and any other relevant information. The role of the adviser is to do three things: to calm the recipient down if necessary, to help them talk about what has happened, and to give them advice on what options are available to them, given the policy.

The adviser is not to conduct an interrogation, to find out whether the recipient is telling the truth, whether she is 'over the top', to decide whether she should be feeling this way or to make any other pejorative judgement; rather she or he must believe the recipient's account of how she feels.

The adviser must be familiar with the policy document and the options open to the victim. The advice given will depend to a large extent on the degree to which the recipient is upset, her status within the organization, the harasser and his status, the frequency of the harassment, the type of harassment (see Chapter 2: Defining Sexual Harassment), and where and when it happened. As a result of hearing about the incident the adviser will need to make suggestions as to the way forward.

Complaints procedure 1 (informal)

The first probable course of action is for the adviser to suggest that the recipient talk to the perpetrator herself and ask him to stop the behaviour. Empowering recipients to act themselves is important. You can help her decide what to do by detailing the four different informal approaches, (see Chapter 12: Challenging the Harasser).

a) confronting the harasser face-to-face

b) writing the harasser a letter

c) confronting the harasser over the telephone

d) offering to accompany her to confront the harasser face-to-face

If the recipient feels she may be able to do one of these things, explore with her the way in which she might proceed (see Chapter 12 Challenging the Harasser). It is important that you allow the recipient to make up her own mind. By all means encourage her, support her and empower her, but do not make up her mind for her. That might leave her even more helpless and vulnerable.

If she is unwilling to act in this way because, for example, she is too frightened, he is too senior to her, she is too self-conscious, she thinks the harasser will take revenge or lose his temper, or he feels it will make the situation worse, then it is not worth proceeding with this suggestion.

Complaints procedure 2 (informal)

This second procedure only applies if it has been established that the recipient feels that she is unable to confront the harasser herself. The reasons for her deciding against direct confrontation will be varied (see above). However, something has to be done.

This informal method requires a senior member of staff, the alleged harasser's line manager, or the personnel manager to speak to him on an informal level. No notes are kept in the alleged harasser's file and no further action is taken as a result of this action. As a senior officer or personnel manager you are seeking to find a swift resolution, stop the behaviour from being repeated and enable working relationships between all parties to be resumed.

Before the senior officer speaks with the alleged harasser it is important that the recipient writes down the complaint, dates and signs it. The adviser may assist in this process. The senior officer will read the complaint and ask to see the alleged harasser. The alleged harasser will be informed why he is being asked to attend the meeting and that if he chooses he can be accompanied by a friend.

The aim of the meeting is to try and resolve the situation. It will be stated that the meeting itself, the conversations, the resolution and the allegations will be subject to confidentiality.

In the first stage of the interview with the harasser, the aim is to try and make explicit what happened. Many cases of sexual harassment occur because the alleged perpetrator believes that his actions are, whilst frisky, allowable. He also believes that the recipient will receive them in the spirit with which they were intended, as a 'bit of a laugh', or, that, as the office Romeo, he is just trying to make the 'girls' feel wanted. So it is important to extract the facts: for example, that he did hug her, he did tell her a dirty joke. It does not matter what his intentions were at the time, or what he thought the recipient wanted/liked/said.

If the alleged harasser acknowledges that what the recipient described did take place then it is likely that a resolution can be effected fairly quickly. Whilst there may well be conflicting views about motive and feelings the aim is for the harasser to agree that what the recipient said happened did, and that she has a right to her own feelings about that incident. Again, it doesn't matter what he liked or wanted. It is she who has been offended.

Often, once this point has been explained, the harasser is prepared to offer an apology. It may be necessary, however, for the senior officer to suggest that this be done, but it will be also be important to state that it is expected that professional relations will resume immediately, that no victimization will take place and that confidentiality will be respected. You may need to inform him that victimization is unlawful under the Sex Discrimination Act (1975) (see Chapter 11: The Role of Management).

Once the apology has been offered it may be that the harasser is somewhat shocked by the ordeal. This is perfectly reasonable. Behaviour which he has used for years, communication patterns which he has relied on for a bit of a laugh, have got him into trouble. He may well feel somewhat shaky and need a shoulder to cry on, not necessarily now, but in a few days when the incident has sunk in.

During the meeting it is important that the senior officer does not actually accuse the harasser of sexual harassment. To accuse someone of being a sexual harasser with no other evidence than one person's word is to have a person convicted before their trial. Stating that a person is a sexual harasser, when you are in a senior position, on the basis of second-hand information, has the effect of taking information from the private domain into the public arena, which could constitute grounds for a case of libel or slander brought against you, the manager.

This, however, does not preclude you, as the senior officer, from approaching the alleged perpetrator and saying that the victim has come to you and told you that from her point of view this is what she thought happened and that she wants the alleged behaviour to stop. It will also be important that you inform him that this is part of an informal process, that you are happy to listen to his version of events, and you are seeking a conciliation and resolution immediately in order that the matter can be forgotten and that working relationships resume as soon as possible.

Complaints procedure 3 (formal)

The formal complaints procedure needs to be followed on occasions where the nature of the alleged sexual harassment is more serious than that dealt with in steps one or two and breaches the company's code of conduct. Or this step may be taken directly if, after the initial meeting, the harasser claims that the allegation is untrue, or that he wasn't even at the place where she claimed the harassment took place. In the face of a categorical denial, the organization has no other course than to proceed along formal lines.

The method then is for the alleged harassment to be brought to the attention of a senior member of staff. On the grounds that the harasser is denying the incident and accusation, and the recipient is claiming she has been harassed, a senior manager organizes an investigation.

The person who has acted as the adviser should not be the investigator. Nor should the managing director be the investigator, as he or she will need to make a decision after the investigation has been completed. It is very important for the investigator be as impartial as possible, that he or she is neither a friend nor a colleague of either party, nor in the pocket of the managing director, but a person regarded by other employees as a trustworthy, honest broker. The role of the investigator is to collect as much information as quickly as possible from a variety of sources. He or she will interview people connected with the incident and known to the recipient and the alleged harasser.

Once the evidence has been collected, the investigator will write a report which will be given to the managing director/chair of the board/a panel or the person dealing with the case. This person/panel will make a decision as to what will happen, based on the information collected. In a case where there is no direct corroborative evidence, sexually harassing behaviour may be inferred in the case of an individual who has been the object of numerous allegations of such behaviour, or similar behaviour. Depending on the nature of the harassment the perpetrator will be dismissed, moved from the position he holds to another in a different area to that of the recipient, or be warned. He may be offered counselling.

Complaints procedure 4 (formal)

This final step may be reached either directly, because the harassment was particularly severe and the recipient wishes to have direct legal action taken, or indirectly. By indirectly I mean that the recipient will have gone through the procedures described above but with no satisfactory resolution having been made because she is not happy with the investigator's findings or the managing director's/panel's decision.

Once all the informal procedures have been undertaken the time has probably been reached when the only option is to take the case to an Industrial Tribunal. The recipient may want compensation, her name cleared, the employer found negligent, and the perpetrator found guilty and dismissed. The employer may be liable for compensation if it is found that sexual harassment did occur, that there was no policy, no training of staff, or that the incident was not dealt with effectively.

The recipient may want to handle the case herself (see Chapter 13: Taking a Case to an Industrial Tribunal). She may decide, however, to be professionally represented and wish to talk with her union, the Citizens Advice Bureau, a solicitor, a legal representative, the Industrial Tribunals, the Equal Opportunities Commission or the police for legal advice on the path to take.

By this time the case will be out of the organization's jurisdiction. However, people within the organization may be called to give evidence. It is important for senior managers to make swift and effective preparation to train all staff about sexual harassment.

CHAPTER EIGHT

Countering the Sceptics

Introduction

I claim in the Introduction that sexual harassment is an emotive subject. It becomes even more of an emotive issue when you begin raising awareness in order to bring about the implementation of a policy and grievance procedure. No one, it seems, is neutral. However, it is important for you, as the initiator of such a programme, to be aware yourself of the likely setbacks and possible defences people use in order to scupper your intentions.

This chapter looks at what people may do to hinder attempts to eliminate sexual harassment from the workplace. The first section discusses change and the resistance this brings. The second section gives four brief, common statements offered as reasons for not changing, followed by some considered responses. The last section provides trainers, personnel managers and others concerned about changing behaviour with short statements of fact which are worth remembering for use with difficult employees.

Attitudes to change

Introducing training and education about sexual harassment into an organization essentially means bringing about change. This can well engender negative responses from some in the workforce, who will view the project with suspicion and hostility. After all, they may well be asked to give up what they are comfortable with, to replace it with what is initially unknown and even frightening.

There are changes that individual choose and those that they do not. Of course we feel most comfortable with those we choose. We give them consideration, the person doing the choosing is in control of the situation, deciding the rate at which the change occurs, exactly what changes and what doesn't, and how the change takes place. If we feel we are in control we are usually happier about change.

A change that is foist on us may be one we initially resist for that very reason: we don't necessarily know why we are being asked to change; we may not think it is justified, we don't have any control over the change and we are not sure where it will lead. Statements like: 'I liked it the way it was'; 'there is no reason to change this process; it works': 'the devil you know is better than the devil you don't', are indicative of a person's reluctance to move on or acknowledge that there is any reason to do so.

Denial

This is the first step that people often take in the change process. It is called 'denial'.

Denying that there is a problem with sexual harassment or that something should be done about it is very common. Some people deny that sexual harassment even exists. Some people, if reluctantly conceding that it does, then deny that it's a real problem or that the behaviour is unusual, untoward or offensive to the recipient.

Resistance

The second reaction to the change process is called 'resistance'. Resistance is the phase in which there is often open hostility and antagonism towards both the change and the person or people promoting it. This is typically seen as the 'It can't be done' stage.

People often resist the idea that anything can be done about sexual harassment. For example, they believe that sexual harassment is biologically based: sexual harassers are born, genetically conditioned and testosterone-driven. Training is a waste of time, as are policy statements and grievance procedures. Another common response in this phase is to blame the victim for provocation, being too friendly, not saying 'no', or for wearing the 'wrong' clothes. These are all signs of resistance.

Adaptation

The third stage in the change process is the 'adaptation' phase, when the person is beginning to shift, albeit reluctantly. This phase is characterized by statements such as 'I've got no choice' and 'maybe it will work'. These early signs indicate that change is at last being tolerated although not welcomed.

Acceptance

The last stage is that of acceptance and involvement. Denial is abandoned, resistance is worn down, the idea that change will take place is accepted, and people have been won over and have decided that they need to be involved if they want to be part of the new regime.

Conclusion

These are the stages that some of the employees will go through in an organization in which sexual harassment is to be countered. Actually discussing these four phases at the beginning of the whole process will help individuals understand why they feel the way they do. It will also help the trainer to understand and cope with the inevitable hostility and sabotage likely to come their way from some employees when they begin to introduce an anti-sexual harassment policy and harassment-free workplace practice.

The anxious workplace

The kind of things people say to managers, personnel staff and trainers when they are anxious about the imminent changes likely to occur after training in the area of sexual harassment are exemplified by the statements below. I have taken four of the most common that I have heard from people I have trained. I have then given some possible responses to these people in order to calm their fears, but at the same time without conceding that they are unable to change or that things must stay as they are.

1. Bert Castle, Senior Clerk: 'The problem with all this sexual harassment stuff is that I don't know how to respond to staff anymore. I may say something in all innocence which they see as harassment'.

2. Bob Young, Sales Manager: 'Sexual jokes, innuendoes and sexual comments are all part and parcel of office life. Young trainees and girls just have to get used to it'.

3. Diana Close, Personal Assistant to the Financial Director: 'There really isn't much I can do about it now. The boss has been calling me "Sweetie" since I first got here. I mean I've been working for him for 18 months'.

4. Peg Bishop, Administrative Manager: 'I suppose the problem is that I don't want to hurt his feelings. He is such a nice man really, and has a lovely wife. I know he doesn't mean anything by it. It's just the way he is. I can put up with it. It's better than getting him embarrassed and upset.'

Some possible responses to Bert, Bob, Diana and Peg

1. It would be important to point out to Bert Castle that professional comments and courteous requests are appropriate in the workplace at all times. He doesn't have to worry, because if he maintains these standards he will not be accused of sexual harassment. It may be important to tell him that it is unnecessary to tell jokes, play pranks and regale staff with stories of personal feats and adventures, because this is the workplace and work is supposed to be going on. As a senior clerk, Bert also has a responsibility to others more junior than him, and he may need reminding of this fact. Bert may have to be told to keep his personal stories for his friends out of work hours unless he is absolutely sure and has checked out with the audience that they are happy to hear the tales.

2. Bob Young, a senior manager, is trying to argue that he has the right to decide what should and should not happen in the workplace. What he does not seem to realize is that young trainees and new employees have a right not to be embarrassed, trivialized, humiliated and belittled by jokes, comments, and remarks. They have a right to work in a safe environment and be protected by managers. Sexual jokes, innuendoes and sexual comments may constitute sexual harassment as being a detriment and an example of sex discrimination or indeed become so unpleasant for a member of staff that she takes a case of constructive dismissal to an Industrial Tribunal. Sex discrimination in unlawful under the 1975 Sex Discrimination Act.

Incidentally, it is inappropriate to use the word *girl* for a young woman over the age of 16. Bob should have pointed out to him how patronizing it sounds.

3 Diana Close believes that because she has put up with sexual harassment for 18 months she is not in a position to ask the boss to change his behaviour. Just because he has been calling her patronizing names for 18 months does not mean that she has to put up with it. I would warn her that he may be a little surprised to hear that she does in fact mind that term. But that is no reason to put up with it. One of the reasons for having training and development is to make people become more aware of their behaviour and to change it accordingly. Understanding sexual discrimination and changing women's sometimes passive and negative views about themselves is one of the very positive aspects of this kind of training. Helping women realize that they do not have to put up with patronizing language is extremely important. It is one aspect of an increasing awareness of people's rights.

4 It is important here that you talk to Peg Bishop about her feelings. Has he hurt *her* feelings? Is *she* embarrassed and upset? It is also important that you raise her awareness of the fact that his behaviour is not biologically based and that he could change it if he wanted to. He could stop being patronizing, touching, patting and making sexist comments, but he has to be told, and probably she is the person to do it as she seems to genuinely like him and care for him. Prepare her for the event that he might be a little hurt, but assure her that he won't collapse. It may also be worth pointing out to her that she is being a little over-protective in taking responsibility for a man's unwanted behaviour. She might possibly be putting him in a vulnerable position

vis-à-vis other women, who might not be as polite as Peg and could make a formal complaint, leading to a formal or informal investigation which, in turn, could lead to him being sacked.

Facts and information

In the last two sections we have looked at some of the ways in which the existence of sexual harassment, and in particular training and education about the issue, can be denied, trivialized or ignored. Further, we have discussed how those responsible for instituting training can deal effectively with people who are anxious about change, and those who are unsure of what a sexual harassment-free work environment would look like.

Before you get too despondent, this final section gives managers some facts and information about sexual harassment so that you can be prepared to combat any possible deluge of negative comments and attitudes voiced or rumoured at the start of a development and training programme. They are worth memorizing for future use.

- Sexual harassment is a learned social behaviour and can be unlearned.

- Sexual harassment is not a new phenomenon, it has been going on for decades. It was not until the late 1970s, however, that unwanted attention of this kind was so named.

- Sexual harassment can be difficult to deal with because different people can have different perceptions of the same behaviour. However, it is the right of the aggrieved party to label the behaviour as unwanted.

- There is no one list of behaviours, gestures, words or literature that constitute sexual harassment.

- What is acceptable to one work colleague may not be acceptable to another. Everyone has different thresholds on matters of personal space, touching, dirty jokes, etc., and these different thresholds have to be taken into consideration.

- Because sexual harassment is difficult to define and is contentious, just writing policies and giving them as handouts is not good enough. Education and training programmes are essential to eliminate sexual harassment from the workplace.

- People who claim they have been sexually harassed need, in the first instance, to be supported and offered help and information on how to handle the perpetrator or how to lodge a complaint.

- Sexual harassment often conforms to what is expected of 'macho' males.

- Sexual harassment can be directed at one person or at a group of people; it can have an indirect effect on a person or on a group of people.

- Sexual harassment can encompass touching, looking, grunting, gesturing, as well as 'phone calls, graffiti, pin-ups, printed matter, letters and notes.

CHAPTER NINE

Countering Myths and Misconceptions

Introduction

In the last chapter I discussed one very real problem encountered by managers, trainers and personnel officers attempting to raise awareness of sexual harassment issues in the workplace, that of denials by some who wish to maintain the status quo. Another set of saboteurs make use of misconceptions to substantiate their claim that sexual harassment is not a serious issue or offensive and debilitating behaviour.

It is important to deal with these. But it is also worth making a judicious choice of whom to challenge, when to do so and when to let it pass. If one were to challenge every myth or misconception about sexual harassment, sexism or sexual discrimination life would be exceedingly wearisome and confrontational. This is partly because those challenged usually defend their position and their attitudes in a fairly hostile manner.

Having said that, I once challenged people over sexist jokes made in an after-dinner speech. One speaker was extremely contrite, went pink when I told him I found his 'joke' about secretaries offensive, and said he didn't know why he had told it. However, on the same evening, another speaker who also publicly told a 'joke' about an unmarried mother abused me, saying that this dinner was a private affair and he could tell whatever jokes he liked.

I have always maintained that in the long run education is better than confrontation, although, at the right time, in the right place, confrontation can be extremely effective.

Below are some of the most common myths, to which I have provided some considered responses. It is important that if you are intending to challenge, you have the arguments and justifications to refute them at your fingertips.

Myths and misconceptions

Sexual harassment is not really an important issue. It doesn't hurt anyone.

Your task is to make the speaker understand that far from being a trivial issue, it has far-reaching consequences for all and is an important social issue for four main reasons. First, sexual harassment does hurt. People subjected to sexual harassment experience a wide range of physical and psychological ailments, including headaches, ulcers, depression, tension and other stress-related illnesses.

Second, sexual harassment can have economic consequences for the recipient. A person who is being sexually harassed may decide to hand in their notice, drop out of a course or quit university. This could be detrimental to their career in both the long and the short term.

Third, a consequence of overt sexual harassment, in an organization, is that it has an effect on all the others working there too. If the environment is one in which people do not feel safe, work will not be at its best.

Fourth, the organization itself will suffer financially from unwanted staff turnover, low productivity, poor public image, unnecessary expense of recruitment of new staff, and legal costs and possible compensation payments for a case taken to an Industrial Tribunal. If the harasser is not discovered and dealt with appropriately and effectively, the chances are that another woman will become a recipient of his unwanted sexual attentions.

That wasn't sexual harassment. I was only joking, and she knew I was only messing about. She likes it, anyway.

Many harassers, if asked why they harassed a person, defend their behaviour by saying they thought it was funny, they were having a bit of a joke with the recipient, and they justify their actions further by claiming that the recipient didn't mind. One of the first questions might be is to ask them how they know the woman doesn't mind? Sexual harassment has little to do with what the harasser intends and has everything to do with what the recipient feels. It is also important for harassers to understand that women and men view particular behaviours in very different lights. Further, it is not up to the harasser to decide for her that the woman enjoyed the attention. The bottom line is that if a person believes that they have been sexually harassed, it is up to the harasser and the organization to take the complaint seriously.

Sexual harassment! Don't be ridiculous! It's only natural for men to make a pass at women. You can't change human nature.

Many people think, mistakenly, that men are sexually uncontrollable: if they see a 'pretty face', or a particular part of a woman's body, they cannot resist touching, patting or making a comment. In the Victorian era it was believed, by some, that a man's sexual urge had to be met on demand for him not to go insane, at worst, or be severely affected by it, at least. In fact, sexual harassment, has nothing to do with natural male behaviour. Men are not born knowing how to sexually harass others. Sexual harassment is learned social behaviour, learned within the context of a sexist environment. If sexist practices and sexual discrimination were eradicated, sexual harassment too would stop.

Similarly, sexual harassment hasn't anything to do with sexual attraction, genuine expressions of affection or consensual flirting between employees. It is true that a great many people meet their future partner in the workplace, but these relationships do not begin with unwanted pats, touches, sexual innuendoes or being shown pornographic photographs. Sexual relationships start from consensual behaviour which develops into a mutual relationship. People do not form loving relationships with those who sexually harass them.

Sexual harassment can only be defined as such when there is actual physical contact.

Here the speaker is looking for a watertight definition, which can be tested each time. However, as we have already seen in Chapter 2, there is no clear-cut way of defining sexual harassment. What is done, by whom, when, where and, most importantly, what the recipient feels it to be and how it has affected her, are all questions which need to be considered.

However, one thing is certainly clear: sexual harassment includes a number of different kinds of behaviours, of which touching is only one. There are many other kinds of offensive behaviour which may constitute sexual harassment. It is the recipient of the behaviour who decides whether or not they feel sexually harassed. Behaviour or actions which could constitute sexual harassment can take many forms and include requests for sexual favours, leers, physical contact, sexist remarks, dirty jokes, pin-ups, explicit sexual comments, innuendo and remarks about a person's body. Interestingly, people in positions of power frequently ignore verbal sexual harassment.

They should tell us if they don't like it. If they did we would stop.

This misconception about sexual harassment comes from an assumption that women and men have equal power in the workplace. Not only is that untrue (women earn 67 per cent of men's wages and only occupy approximately 3 per cent of senior executive positions), but also it is hardly fair to expect the recipient of sexual harassment to take responsibility for unwanted behaviour.

Unfortunately one consequence of sexual harassment is to silence women, because they are afraid that if they complain they will be accused of provoking it, that they will be told they have no sense of humour, that they are frigid, liars, are exaggerating, hysterical, or abnormal. Recipients are also afraid of victimization.

That wasn't sexual harassment: I was just paying her a compliment.

This is an exceedingly difficult statement to deal with. Of course, not all compliments constitute sexual harassment. But I think we need to look more deeply at what is involved. First, women are complimented more than men. Second, the compliments that women receive almost invariably are to do with what they are wearing, how their face looks, what their hair is like, how slim or fat they have become since they were last seen, and other personal comments. Rarely do women complain about compliments which focus on their work performance, their expertise, their skilful handling of a delicate situation or other professional work.

[Joan Swann mentions compliments in her book *Girls, Boys and Language* (1992).] [In a study in the U.S. it was found that] women received more compliments than men. Furthermore, while men tended to be complimented by someone older or a superior (for example; a boss complimenting an employee on his work), women could be complimented by anyone. Many compliments to women concerned their appearance. Wolfson gives examples such as a male professor who interrupted a female professor's class to whisper loudly: 'Can I whisper in your ear? I didn't have the chance to tell you this morning how lovely you look.'

[She continues] Compliments, terms of endearment, and comments on someone's appearance are normally intended to be pleasant, but they also serve as a reminder that a woman's appearance is available to be commented upon and that the person giving the compliment is in a position to pass judgement. (Swann, 1993, pp.31-32).

It must always be remembered that sexual harassment is in the eye of the person receiving the compliment, not in the eye of the person passing it. If a person feels uncomfortable with a comment made, it is an indication that it was inappropriate, and the person giving it should stop immediately, rather than berate her for being difficult, muttering that it must be the wrong time of the month, or suggesting she is menopausal.

It is also important to understand that each of us has a different level of tolerance. Behaviour which might be accepted by one person may not be acceptable in the same way by another person. To a great extent giving and receiving compliments are context-bound and are dependent on the relationship between the recipient and the perpetrator, as well as other variables such as status, authority, position, etc. Also it is important to recognize that behaviour which might be accepted in more personal situations can be inappropriate in the workplace.

Look, what I was doing was only a bit of fun. It wasn't meant to be taken seriously. They should have a sense of humour.

This statement implies that sexual harassment is 'harmless fun'. It is not. It is degrading and humiliating. Sexual harassment means being treated as a sex object, not as a worker/employee. Some people confuse sexual harassment with flirtation. It is important to make the distinction. Flirtation can be harmless fun. But, the prerequisite is that the interest be mutual and no intimidation involved. It is not fun or funny to be subjected to unwanted behaviour. It is not 'harmless' to harass anyone verbally, or to pinch or pat them.

Women who dress provocatively can't be sexually harassed!

The argument about provocation has been going on for decades. In the American magazine *Harper's Weekly* (year unknown) an article appeared which shed new light on the issue. What seems to be a normal cross-examination changes our view of the victim from a recipient who deserves sympathy into someone who 'asked for it'. The evident ridiculousness of this dialogue can illuminate how sexual harassment is often viewed as being the fault of the recipient.

Q: Mr Smith, were you held up at gun point on the corner of First and Main?

A: Yes.

Q: Did you struggle with the robber?

A: No.

Q: Why not?

A: He was armed.

Q: Then you made a conscious decision to comply with his demands rather than resist?

A: Yes.

Q: Did you scream? Cry out?

A: No, I was afraid.

Q: I see. Have you ever been held up before?

A: No.

Q: Have you ever given money away?

A: Yes, of course.

Q: And you did so willingly?

A: What are you getting at?

Q: Well, let's put it like this Mr Smith. You've given money away in the past. In fact you have a reputation for philanthropy. How can we be sure you weren't *contriving* to have your money taken by force?

A: Listen if I wanted...

Q: Never mind. What time did this hold-up take place?

A: About 11.00 pm.

Q: You were out on the streets at 11.00 pm? Doing what?

A: Just walking.

Q: Just walking? You know that it's dangerous being out on the street late at night. Weren't you aware that you could have been held up?

A: I hadn't thought about it.

Q: What were you wearing?

A: Let's see ... a suit. Yes, a suit.

Q: An expensive suit.

A: Well - yes. I'm a successful lawyer, you know.

Q: In other words, Mr Smith, you were walking around the streets late at night in a suit that practically advertized the fact that you might be a good target for easy money, isn't that so? I mean, if we didn't know better, Mr Smith, we might even think that you were asking for this to happen, mightn't we?

An interesting twist: the victim of a robbery is made out to have provoked it, and the robber is not really a criminal, more an opportunist. What is interesting is that this is often the kind of response a woman receives if she has been subject to a sexual assault, attack or sexual harassment. She is blamed for having been in the wrong place, at the wrong time, wearing the wrong clothes and so on.

Data on incidents of sexual harassment show that it has nothing to do with age, looks, body size, clothes, location or time. Anyone can be sexually harassed, although the majority of recipients are women and the majority of perpetrators are men.

No one 'asks' to be humiliated, threatened and embarrassed. What a person wears, where they walk, the time they go out, and who they go out with is their affair and does not give anyone licence to sexually harass.

If you ignore sexual harassment it will go away.

The implication appears to be that the tormentor will ultimately get bored, give up and try another victim. This does not seem to be true. Research suggests that ignoring sexual harassment only makes it worse. The reason is that sexual harassment is behaviour based on the abuse of power and as such is used as a mechanism to control the recipient. Remaining silent about such behaviour does not stop it. In fact often the opposite occurs. The perpetrator believes that the messages are not being received, so the unwanted attention gets worse or more frequent.

If women go into places where they are not welcome then they should expect to be sexually harassed.

This myth supports the belief that boys and men have rights to commandeer certain places as reserves for men only, or for male-type behaviour only. In these reserves they can treat interlopers, i.e. women, disrespectfully, in a discriminating manner and with abuse. Their arguments are usually along the lines of: if they don't like it in here they don't have to come in.

However, this is now unlawful treatment under the Sex Discrimination Act (1975): it is illegal to discriminate against people on the grounds of their sex, in areas of employment, education, the provision of housing, goods and services, and advertizing. Employees have the right to be respected wherever they go within the workplace. They also have the right to be provided with equal access to all the work facilities.

Sexual harassment! I wish I could get some!

Here is an attempt at trivializing sexual harassment. However, I believe the person who makes this statement has mixed up the terms 'harassment' and 'attention'. Sexual harassment is unwanted. Sexual attention is wanted. People do not like being sexually harassed. Do people like being bullied? Sexual harassment is akin to bullying and not the same as sexual attention. Many people like sexual attention and use many devices to get it. One is to wear particular clothes. However, this does not mean that the person who is wearing attractive clothes wants sexual attention from you! Remember, sexual attention can be fun, sexy, intimate and clandestine but, above all, it is *wanted*. Sexual harassment is an unacceptable form of social interaction, is intimidating, frightening or humiliating.

Sexual harassment my foot! Boys will be boys, you know!

One of the problems with sexual harassment is that it is seen to be a normal and natural way for men, in particular, to behave. Of course, young men and women have sexual desires. However, as sexual harassment has little to do with sexual pleasure, but is rather an expression of power and domination and is perpetrated often by the same man on many different women in one office or workplace, to claim that sexual harassment is a result of men's sexual appetite is fallacious, antiquated and incorrect.

All the women I know go along with it so they must be enjoying it.

This myth comes from a position of ignorance. Either the person hasn't spoken to many women about this behaviour or if they have they don't hear what the women are actually saying. With all the media attention regarding the issue it would be a most non-perceptive person who hasn't come across an incident.

However, one of the well-known problems associated with being a victim of sexual harassment is that the recipient often remains silent. They are unlikely to speak out to ask the person to stop, especially if that person is in a position of power over them. Also, women have been taught not to object to male behaviour for they have learned that this is normal and natural. Further, because of their training as females, women often have different ways of expressing discomfort and embarrassment. Many women smile, giggle, look down, play with their hair or fiddle with their clothes. These actions do not mean they are enjoying the situation. Men are much more likely to speak out about things they don't like.

CHAPTER TEN

Your Role as an Adviser

Introduction

Each company, university, or workplace should have trained personnel available to help and advise people who have been sexually harassed. This chapter looks at the role that person might have and what they could expect to do if a recipient needed their help.

Appointing an adviser for recipients of sexual harassment

The number of trained personnel needed will depend on the number of employees working there, the arrangement of the workplace (if it has more than one work site), the type of employees (are there many different levels, skilled, unskilled, race groups, ages, etc.?), as well as how well integrated the departments are.

Depending on the employees there are, you may wish to have personnel trained for particular groups, for example:

- Administrative officers

- Students

- Shopfloor workers

- Part-time staff

- Managers

- Technical staff

- Professional staff

- Non-professional staff

As most people who suffer sexual harassment are women it is appropriate for most of the advisers to be women. However, the adviser should not be the most senior woman, for two reasons.

First, people who have been sexually harassed often do not feel comfortable talking with someone who is in a position of power or authority.

Second, if the adviser is in senior management or is a senior officer, it may fall to her to be involved in conducting the investigation or having other responsibilities in dealing with grievances, discipline, training, etc.

The role of the adviser

As incidents of sexual harassment are painful experiences it is important that the person to whom the recipient first speaks be as sensitive and as open as possible to the claims made. The adviser must understand the issues which underlie sexual harassment, be aware of how difficult it often is for the recipient to make a complaint, especially if the perpetrator is their boss, or a respected male colleague, as well as how guilty or dirty they may feel for their assumed part in this incident.

The adviser must also be skilful in listening, hearing and displaying empathy. When the recipient of harassment arrives at the door, or catches you in the corridor, or rings you up to ask if she can have a word with you, it is important that you, if at all possible, provide her with your time and support immediately. If this is impossible because you have a meeting or appointment that you cannot cancel, then make sure you arrange a time and a place in the immediate future. You may suggest that when you have finished whatever you had to do, you will come and find her. Remember, it may have taken her weeks of turmoil to have plucked up courage to approach you. You do not want this opportunity to be missed.

The recipient

It is likely that when a recipient of harassment first comes to see you that the situation will be highly charged emotionally. The victim of harassment may be extremely angry, frightened or upset, and may exhibit a variety of emotional signals: swearing, crying, silence or hysterics. Each person has a different way of coping with offensive behaviour. It is also not uncommon for distressed victims to smile and to look relaxed as they tell of their experiences. Be sure that you do not judge how they feel from their countenance alone, as victims of offensive behaviour can have a variety of expressions and demeanours.

The first step is to let her calm down. If she is weeping uncontrollably, some ways of letting her take control of her emotions are to pass her a box of tissues, get her a cup of coffee and say things like: 'There is no hurry. Take all the time you need. When you are ready we can talk then.'

If she is angry, swearing and banging the table, suggest she sits down, offer her a drink and be prepared to let her anger run its course before you ask her about the incident.

It is important that the recipient be given the time she needs to tell you what has happened and that she is not confronted with a barrage of questions or forms to fill in. After she has calmed down, she may need to get her thoughts in order, and hear some encouraging and positive words from you before she is willing to disclose the information. She may need to test out that you will be receptive to her claim. It will be important that you say things and indicate non-verbally that you believe that she has been upset and you can help her decide what she wants to do next. It is essential for reasons of privacy, trust and confidentiality that you are not disturbed by telephone calls or interrupted by other personnel.

What of the adviser's reaction and feelings?

What the recipient has to tell you may be highly personal and embarrassing for them and for you. For example, the incident may be as degrading as the one cited in the BBC programme, *Making Advances*. There a boss asked his secretary if she had clean hands. When she said 'yes', he told her that was good because he wanted her to hold his penis. This type of sexual harassment is not unusual, but it is the adviser's role to remain calm herself, to listen sympathetically and not to show disgust, horror or outrage.

It may be that the incident described makes you feel angry, dirty, embarrassed, outraged, or humiliated too. On the other hand you may have problems with the veracity of the recipient's story. You may find it impossible to believe that the male perpetrator she is naming, who is a colleague of yours, could do this to a woman. The perpetrator may even be a friend. It is of no help if you lose control of yourself, cry, get angry or storm out of the room, or say you really can't believe that this man with whom you may have worked for years, would do that sort of thing. You must remain calm in order to help the recipient.

Another problem which may arise is that her experience might bring back to you an incident which happened in your own life, which you may not have dealt with. Now is not the time to do this. Wait until this woman has calmed down, you have given her advice and she has left your office before you get support for yourself.

It is also sometimes a temptation to tell recipients about your own or another person's experience of sexual harassment, or for you to compare their experiences with others you may know about because you think it will make them feel better. This will not be helpful to them at the moment, although in due course it may be important that they do understand that they are not the only person to whom this has happened, either in a general way, or specifically from the hands of this perpetrator.

At the end of the session you may feel wrung out. It is an emotionally draining process to listen, support and give advice to a person who is very upset. It is therefore important that you have a support network. There may be other 'advisers' in your institution to whom you can talk. Obviously you will not reveal the names of the people concerned. You may also wish to speak with your partner, a friend or relative outside office hours. This will help you off-load some of the tension. Again it is recommended as long as the identity of the persons involved is not revealed.

Handling the situation

It is important, when they first arrive and ask to talk to you, that you believe their interpretation of the experience and assure them that they have acted correctly in coming to you. Give them eye contact, sit in a relaxed and 'open' way and do not give negative or disbelieving non-verbal signals. Do not sit in a 'closed' style with arms and legs crossed tightly, not looking at them and with a disbelieving expression on your face. Do not interrogate them because you are interested in the fine details of their plight. Remember the purpose of their visit is that they need your help.

If at all possible sit with them, not behind a desk or across a room and have the chairs in an informal arrangement. Try not to position them so that they have the sun or a light shining directly in their face.

You may want to thank them for telling you and comment on how difficult it can be to talk to someone about behaviour of this kind.

If they find discussing the incident difficult try asking questions such as:

- Tell me what happened.

- Who was involved?

- When and where did this happen?

- What did you say or do at the time?

- How often has this happened or is this the first time?

- Was there anyone who saw or heard this?

- Have you spoken to anyone else about this incident/these incidents?

- Did you keep a diary or notes about the harassment?

- Is there any other evidence or documentation of the incident?

- How have you been affected by this harassment?

It will not be helpful to the recipient if you conduct an investigation. This is not your job. It will also not help them if you make comments or ask questions which make them feel that in some way they were responsible for the behaviour, or that their complaint is trivial or time-wasting. Try not to ask 'why' questions. These are usually judgmental and imply that the recipient has behaved inappropriately herself.

Naming the behaviour

One of my experiences of working with people in this area is that some do not know what the behaviour they have been subjected to is called. One such woman was an African student called Bernadette, who had come to the UK to study. A student friend of hers had suggested she come to see me. Bernadette's English, whilst academically sound, was neither colloquial nor extensive for it was not her first language. When she arrived in my office she was very quiet and spent some time checking me out. When I began to ask her what had happened her description was full of 'ums' and 'ers' and 'you knows'.

However, whilst the details were sketchy she did give me enough information about her feelings and the unwanted behaviour for me to suggest tentatively: 'It sounds as though what you have experienced is sexual harassment.' Her face looked at me questioningly and she said, 'What is that?' I then explained what sexual harassment was, how offensive it can be, how frightened the recipient may feel, and how silenced they can be made. The conversation continued, and still the information I received was sketchy.

A few days later I took Bernadette to the personnel department of the organization in which the harassment had occurred in order to make a formal complaint. Again the interview was vague and repetitive, yet there was an unmistakable veracity about the account.

We left, having made a half-hearted complaint. Ironically, on the way back to my car an incident occurred which clarified the whole situation. In a line of parked vehicles sat a man, reading what I thought was a map. He beckoned me over. I thought him lost and went to his aid. Far from being lost, he was masturbating under the 'map' on his lap. I quickly stepped back, telling him that this was preposterous behaviour and I would be notifying the police. He jumped out of the car as I took down the registration number and threatened me, but eventually backed away, returned to his vehicle and drove off.

On going back to the path, I was shaking and angry. I looked at Bernadette and asked: 'Did you see what that man was doing? I can't believe that he was masturbating in the middle of the afternoon and thought it all right to invite me to watch'. Bernadette went quiet. 'That is what my tutor did to me when I was in his office', she said.

The point of this example is to signal the need for sensitivity on the part of the adviser to help name behaviour which has been experienced, in this case as sexual harassment, as well as to realize that not all people have the same vocabulary. Bernadette neither knew the phenomenon, sexual harassment, nor did she have the term 'masturbation' to describe the unwanted and offensive behaviour to which she had been subjected.

The policy

Once the story has been told, it is important that you give the recipient the necessary information about making a complaint. She needs to know of the informal and formal procedures and the possible consequences. It is important that you provide sound advice, based on the company's policy, on what she can do next. It is a good idea to give the recipient of sexual harassment a copy of the company policy and the grievance procedure so they can look at it in more detail after they have left you.

The treatment they have suffered may constitute a criminal act. The behaviours which do carry criminal penalties are the following:

- sexual assault/physical assault

- offensive literature

- indecent exposure

- obscene 'phone calls or nuisance letters

- threatening behaviour.

In order to proceed with a police investigation and a successful conviction the likelihood is that the recipient will need corroborative evidence; for example, physical marks such as bruising or cuts, the actual letter/literature or an eye witness(es).

However, if you establish that what happened was a criminal offence, or you think it may constitute a criminal offence, it will be necessary for you to advise the recipient to make a complaint to the police, see a solicitor, contact the Rape Crisis Centre or another organization which is trained to deal with these situations. This does not mean that you now abandon her, rather that she needs more specialized help and advice. She may well benefit from having you as a befriender, supporter and advocate in the background.

Have I been able to help?

Sometimes the nature and extent of the harassment, and the limitation or absence of a sexual harassment policy in an organization, leave you feeling as though you have done nothing to help the woman concerned. I had a case such as this when I was lecturing about sexual harassment one day. At the end of the session a young woman, whom I shall call Jenny, came to talk to me about the persistent sexual harassment she was subjected to by her boss, the managing director of a small government office.

We discussed various possibilities. Confronting him. No. Writing him a letter. No. Making a 'phone call to him, at home in the evening when he would be unable to retaliate if his wife was in the room. No. Contacting her union. She didn't belong to one. Talking to a colleague in the office. None would be supportive.

At the end of the discussion I felt that I had been of no use in helping her. Her main concern, and therefore her reluctance to do anything, was that she was frightened this would give her boss the opportunity to sack her. Times were hard and she was worried that she would be unable to get another job. I was at a loss. Finally I suggested that she keep a diary, just for personal use, and document what he said, where he touched her and the effect it had on her work.

About three months later she rang me at my office. The harassment had got worse. She had that morning been to the doctor, who had given her time off because she was suffering from stress. She was distraught. Again, after a few minutes of talking with her, I realized that she was still unable to do anything about the harassment directly. I asked her if she had told the doctor the reason for the stress. She said that she hadn't. The only thing I could suggest was that she return to the doctor, tell him the cause of the stress and have him record the reason on her medical notes. I said that if she ever brought a case to an Industrial Tribunal, those notes might be invaluable evidence.

About two months later I received a letter from Jenny. It said:

> I have been meaning to write to you for some time, and apologize for the delay. I wanted to thank you for the help you gave me last November when I was being sexually harassed by my managing director.
>
> I did speak to him without using the technical terminology and he has complied with my wishes (although he occasionally lapses). He did graduate then to verbal abuse and bullying. I recently approached him about this and, again, he is complying with my wishes with the occasional lapse.
>
> The main thing is that he has accepted what I've said and is making an effort. I could not possibly have done this without your support and cannot thank you enough.

There are two points to be made here. The first is that, as advisers, we are sometimes not aware of the help or support we have given. In this case I thought I had been unable to suggest anything positive at all. The letter shows that this was not the case. The second is how important it is to allow the recipient to resolve the incident at her own pace. In this example the sexual harassment got worse before it got better. Sometimes this is inevitable if we are committed to empowering recipients to deal with it themselves.

Protecting the adviser

Advisers who are working with recipients of harassment need support too. To listen to cases of unwanted sexual advances, distress and trauma can be extremely depressing. Advisers, therefore, need to have the ear of a person with whom they can discuss cases; not in terms of 'who', but in terms of 'what'.

Rape, sexual assault and incest

Once an advisory service has been established, it is likely that cases other than those of sexual harassment will be reported. It is important that those people acting as advisers are clear about the demarcation of their role. Remember, they are not trained counsellors and therefore are not in a position to deal with cases such as rape and sexual assault. They are also not trained to deal with incidents which elicit memories of sexual abuse as children. All these cases need professional people to deal with them. It is important, however, that the adviser does not just abandon victims of these crimes, but provides them with the names and 'phone numbers of people or organizations to which they can go.

CHAPTER ELEVEN

The Role of Management

Introduction

This chapter looks at how management can deal with sexual harassment. It is divided into two main sections. The first describes the proactive and reactive roles. A sample case is given with suggestions as to how a manager might deal with it. The example is hypothetical; no two cases are ever the same, and the suggestions given are just that. Each case must be considered on its own merits. Most are complicated and need careful thought before acting, although delaying action for too long may be disastrous. The second section contains a fictional case for managers to test their own skills, together with some suggestions as to how it might have been handled.

The manager's role

Sexual harassment can be unlawful if it constitutes sexual discrimination in the workplace. It is usually the employer who is taken to an Industrial Tribunal and if the case is found he is liable.

The Sex Discrimination Act (1975) states:

> s.41(2)6.10 A person (a principal) is liable for any act done with his authority (whether express or implied, and whether given before or after the act) by his agent: and an employer is liable for any act done, with or without his knowledge or approval, by one of his employees

in the course of his employment. In these situations the agent or the employee is treated as having aided his principal or employer. In other words, the principal and the agent, and the employer and the employee, are liable for the unlawful act.

In any organization managers and supervisors have an important role to play, ensuring that the workplace is free from sexual harassment and that all the employees understand what behaviours constitute sexual harassment, know whom they can turn to for help and from whom they can reasonably expect support and correct information following a complaint. Managers also have the task of ensuring that incidents which come to their notice are dealt with fairly, efficiently, effectively and immediately. Failure to fulfil these tasks reflects negatively on the managers concerned, as well as possibly breaching employer responsibilities.

Cases of sexual harassment which are drawn to the attention of managers by workers, but subsequently ignored, played down or mishandled, often end up in an Industrial Tribunal. One such case is that of a young woman who was sexually harassed by her line manager. When she informed her union of what was happening, the union representative and the alleged harasser sought an interview with her. At the interview she was told that she was too sensitive, that the boss had been joking and that he didn't mean it, that the young woman should have known what men were like, and that she should give her boss another chance. The company concerned even offered her £100 to keep silent about the case. The case was eventually taken to an Industrial Tribunal and the young woman was awarded over £7,000. The line manager was sacked. (There used to be a ceiling of compensation on sexual discrimination cases. This has now been lifted.)

Managers and supervisors can play a significant role in implementing the organization's policy, in three ways. First, their own behaviour should demonstrate equality, fairness and leadership. Their conduct during meetings, conversations on the 'phone, in the lunch queue, at the end-of-year staff party and organizing staff generally should be appropriate and professional at all times.

Second, managers can play a proactive role in their institution at two levels. At one level they can organize on-going training and education for all staff in the area of sexual harassment. They can also ensure that staff new to the organization have an opportunity and are encouraged to go on an induction course. At another level they can ensure that the work environment is free from sexual harassment. Some of the ways they can do this is to have posters on the wall advertising this work area as a harassment-free zone, and they can tackle any instances that they witness, saying; 'I don't think that is very appropriate behaviour for the workplace', or: 'If I were Anne, I would have you for sexual harassment for doing that'.

Third, managers can ensure that groups of people who are particularly vulnerable, such as first-time workers, women returners, gay men and women, black women, women from ethnic minority groups, divorced, widowed or separated women, and disabled women, are provided with support at times when they are most at risk.

Managers may have the task of writing, implementing and disseminating a policy statement which all staff can understand. It is often beneficial, although time-consuming, to allow a generous period for development of the policy, in order that it can be read and commented on by all groups of workers in the organization. A policy written by a manager who has used no consultative process is likely to be wooden and authoritarian, distant, and not 'owned' by those who are to respect and work within it. Furthermore, the language must be understandable by all employees. Once written and implemented, a policy needs monitoring, updating, reviewing and re-working as the organization changes its attitude to the phenomenon. A manager can take responsibility for this.

Managers must be familiar with the policy's grievance procedure. They must be able to discuss with recipients what to do if someone approaches them with a complaint. The process for making a complaint must be easy to understand and use for if it is too tortuous or frightening recipients will have no faith in the policy working, or in the manager's ability to resolve the situation.

Managers will need to appoint and train advisers for recipients of harassment who are sensitive, caring, supportive and understanding of the issues (see Chapter 10: Your Role as an Adviser). Equally, managers and supervisors may also have individuals coming to them for advice. They need to show empathy and respect to these people and perhaps examine their own beliefs and assumptions, and question their preconceptions and biases in the area of equal opportunities, racism, sexism, disablement and to potential targets of discrimination.

It is also a manager's role to ensure that sexist behaviour is stopped, for sexism leads quite often to sexual harassment. The flaunting of page three photographs, the telling of smutty jokes, and sexual asides must all be questioned and challenged. A manager who remains silent can be seen to have condoned the sexist behaviour.

Victimization

Managers have a role in protecting an employee who makes a claim against another worker or boss. Within the Sex Discrimination Act (1975) is a clause which protects people who make a complaint from victimization.

2.13 The Act also defines as discrimination the victimisation of a person because that person has, for example, asserted his or her rights under the Act or the Equal Pay Act. Victimisation arises where, in any situations to which the Act applies, a person (*the discriminator*) treats another person of the same sex (*the person victimized*) less favourably that he treats, or would treat, other persons on the ground that the person victimised has done (or intends to do, or is suspected of having done or intending to do) any of the following:

(a) brought proceedings against the discriminator or anyone else under the Sex Discrimination Act or Equal Pay Act;

(b) given evidence or information in connection with proceedings brought under either Act by another person against the discriminator or anyone else;

(c) otherwise done anything under, or by reference to, either Act in relation to the discriminator or anyone else (e.g. by giving evidence or information to the Equal Opportunities Commission during the course of formal investigation); or

(d) alleged that the discriminator or anyone else has committed an act which (whether or not this is expressly stated) would constitute a contravention of the Sex Discrimination Act or give rise to a claim under the Equal Pay Act

Even if the complaint is, in time, found to be groundless, no victimization of the complainant must take place if the complaint was submitted in good faith. People involved in an investigation or called to give evidence on the part of the complainant or the respondent are also protected by the victimization clause.

Managers are responsible for nipping in the bud behaviour which is inappropriate in the workplace. It is not in the organization's best interest to leave a potential case of sexual harassment festering and wait until a complaint is made. The harassment needs to be stopped the moment the manager becomes aware of an incident. She or he may become aware of it through their own observations, or by having it drawn to their attention. Ignoring the situation is not only harmful to the recipient, the harasser and the workplace in general, it is also unlawful for a manager in a position of responsibility not to respond.

Sensitivity and extreme care will need to be exercised when approaching parties if no complaint has been made. In the event that the sexual behaviour is consensual and mutual, as a manager you may still wish to advise those concerned that their behaviour is inappropriate in working hours and may constitute sexual harassment for a third party or indirect sexual harassment (see Chapter 2: Defining Sexual Harassment).

The manager may need to advise contract staff, consultants and workers such as emergency plumbers about the general code of practice operating in the workplace. For instance, before hiring window cleaners it may be appropriate to inform the manager of the cleaning company that your organization does not tolerate the sexual harassment of staff whilst contractors are cleaning the windows.

Dealing with a case of sexual harassment

Depending on the organization's grievance procedure, the manager may be responsible for handling cases of sexual harassment her or himself.

A case of harassment which is drawn to your attention by a recipient is not sexual harassment until it is proven so. This means that, as a manager sorting out an informal case, it is not appropriate to accuse the alleged harasser of sexual harassment before an investigation has taken place.

If the nature of the sexual harassment is of Type 1 or Type 2 (see Chapter 2: Defining Sexual Harassment), it may be appropriate for you to approach the alleged harasser directly. The purpose of your approach will not be to accuse him of sexual harassment; rather it will be to ascertain whether particular behaviour did happen.

Let me give an example. A secretary, Sue Brown, comes to you and tells you that each time she takes dictation from her line manager, Ed Smith, he makes sexual innuendoes or unwanted suggestions. Sometimes they are about her private life, of which he knows very little, so they are all assumptions, sometimes they are about her clothes, her make-up and her hair, and at other times they are 'what if' statements, such as 'what if you were to come to Brussels with me on my next assignment'.

Confronting Ed Smith with the accusation: 'You have been sexually harassing Sue Brown', is not appropriate. In this country people are presumed innocent until proved guilty. No investigation has taken place; no accusations should be made. If a manager were to accuse the alleged harasser, this could result in being accused of defamation, libel or slander.

However, you must do something. To do nothing may be unlawful. Approach Ed Smith and ask him to come to your office at such and such a time. He may bring a friend or colleague with him. Tell him that you wish to discuss an allegation against him that has been made by another worker.

At the meeting you warn him of the confidential aspect of this meeting and of the victimization clause in the Sex Discrimination Act (1975). You tell him that an informal complaint has been lodged against him and that you wish to resolve it as quickly and fairly as possible. He may wish to know the precise allegation, and this you can tell him.

Once you have told Ed what has been claimed he may display the following concerns and emotions or behaviour:

- shock that an accusation has been made

- extreme anger with you and the recipient

- joke about it

- trivialize the importance of it

- blame the recipient

- say he doesn't understand what has happened

- demand to speak to the recipient

- concern about his reputation

- fear of dismissal, demotion, his wife finding out, etc.

Ed Smith may also say things like:

- I treat her the same as I treat the others. I don't give her special treatment.

- It's about time the company got rid of her. I knew she was a trouble maker.

- Look, I was only trying to make her feel at home. I can't believe this is happening to me.

- I only meant it as a joke.

- She never did have a sense of humour. If she can't take that sort of thing, she shouldn't be working here.

- She really does have personal problems!

- No wonder she isn't married/I feel sorry for her old man.

- She asked for it. You should see what she was wearing!

- I treat her the same as I treat the others. I don't give her special treatment.

These are all quite common reactions to an allegation of sexual harassment. None of them means that he didn't do what has been charged, only that how he saw the behaviour is clearly very different to the view of the recipient.

However, despite his reaction, he may accept that he has sometimes made little 'jokes' and 'teased' Sue about going to Brussels with him, and 'yes', he does make remarks about her clothes and hair. If this is the case, the matter can be tied up almost directly. What you have here is a mismatch between what he thinks he is doing and what she hears and feels.

Her feelings are completely justifiable. She has the right not to be teased, or have her body and clothes commented on, and she should not have to listen to jokes made about her. He is in a position of power over her and she may fear for her job, her career, and a good reference should she wish to leave the company, if she does not respond positively to Ed's behaviour. She is not peculiar, frigid, or being difficult. Her job is to be a secretary to this man. He has the responsibility to treat her with respect and dignity. This is not happening. It is immaterial what he thinks his intentions were. The upshot of it is that she finds it embarrassing, humiliating and degrading. The behaviour must stop.

In a situation such as this, whilst Ed Smith may be a little surprised and cross that Sue Brown has made a complaint against him, the manager must tell him to stop. He must also be told that professional working relations must be resumed as quickly as possible. If these conditions are agreed to by the harasser, no further formal action need to taken; all that is required is an informal monitoring of the situation. No record need be kept, no one else informed.

The situation will obviously be more difficult than this if the alleged harasser completely denies the recipient's allegations. If this was the case with Ed Smith, he would need to be told at the first meeting that a full investigation will be organized and the company's grievance procedure adopted. Ed would need to be told about confidentiality and victimization.

You, as the manager, may be required to conduct a formal investigation and to report your findings to a panel or the managing director, depending on who pronounces on the case. It is important to note that in a case where there is no corroborative evidence, in many instances it is possible to infer sexually harassing behaviour by an individual from other occasions on which similar behaviour was evidenced. This is often because sexual harassment has little to do with the person being harassed. Harassers are often serial harassers, 'joking', 'teasing', commenting on a woman's body, making sexual innuendoes, sexist remarks and offensive noises to a whole range of women.

Some principles for managers to bear in mind:

- Harassers are not the ones to decide whether or not sexual harassment has taken place.

- Harassers need a non-confrontational approach in the first instance.

- Harassers need to understand that it is their behaviour which is not acceptable, not them as people.

- Harassers need to change their perception of others vis-à-vis themselves.

- Harassing behaviour is about power not sexual attraction.

- Harassment occurs when there is a power imbalance; factors involved include age, status, group size, and the dominant culture.

- Harassers often have power to hire, fire or use coercive measures.

The aim of the talk with the alleged perpetrator is to find out their side of the story. If offence has been caused, you are seeking for an apology to be made, the unwanted behaviour to stop and normal working relations to be resumed as soon as possible.

SOME POINTS TO REMEMBER:

1. This is an alleged offence.

2. You should take an educational, not a punitive stance.

3. You should inform the alleged harasser of the allegation, giving as much detail as possible.

4. Give a fair hearing to their story. Then try to corroborate facts.

5. Do not accuse or antagonize, arouse defensive reactions, be sarcastic or moralistic.

6. If it is accepted that particular behaviour has happened, encourage the perpetrator to acknowledge that, irrespective of intention or perception, the recipient has been offended/embarrassed, etc.

7. Encourage the perpetrator to co-operate in understanding the recipient's complaint, and to learn from this incident.

8. Offer various options for action

   - an apology; written or verbal

   - a promise that the behaviour will not be repeated

   - a promise that they will reassess their own behaviour

   - a promise that they will leave the recipient alone.

9. Explain that no victimization of the complainant must occur.

10. Explain that confidentiality must be respected.

11. Give advice on the institution's sexual harassment policy and discuss various options for this person to further their understanding of the issues.

12. Offer them a listening ear if they need further support.

Activity: try out your managerial skills

As a manager in your organization, you are asked to deal with the following allegation of sexual harassment.

Jane Black claims that Andy Green sexually harassed her, but Andy says that they are really good mates, that he didn't mean anything by his behaviour, she provoked him and got what she asked for, and she is playing hard to get.

Jane's side of the experience. How would you respond to her story?

'It depends what you mean - did we get on? Sort of. I mean the work that we did usually went well, although he often got angry and then he would shout. But afterwards he would ask me to go to the pub to patch things up.

'I didn't really want to go, but I suppose it was his way of saying sorry. When he started telling me jokes and things I thought they were one-offs. I mean I didn't tell him to stop because he only told me them occasionally. And anyway I thought he was just like that, you know, just the odd dirty joke.

'I didn't know what to say when it began to get worse. You see sometimes he was ok. But then it would start again. I didn't want to offend him. I don't know how you can say, 'keep your hands off' without upsetting things. And we had a project that we were involved in together. I tried to show him I didn't like it. I would move away and go quiet. Then I began to wear trousers so that he would stop commenting about my legs. It didn't stop him though.

'This was my first job after university. I had been unemployed for 15 months. I needed the money and I liked the job. I was frightened that if I told Mr Hedges, my line manager, I would get the sack if I complained, or be seen as a trouble maker.

'It was when he started ringing me at home that I realized he was getting more serious.

'Then one morning he asked me if I had any tissues. I had a box on the shelf behind my desk. I told him he could come and get them. He grabbed me from behind, tipped my chair back and demanded a kiss. I hated it.'

Andy's side of the experience. How would you respond to his story?

'But it's ridiculous to say that I sexually harassed her. We are good mates, like an old married couple. Yes, we have the odd fight, but then we'd kiss and make up.

'She never said anything, she never asked me to stop. I think she is strong minded enough that if she hadn't liked it she would have said. Anyway what I did was hardly a crime.

'She's joking. Look, it's personal stuff anyway. I don't think you need to get involved. Really, I will handle it.

'You can't believe this. Look, you don't understand. I was only trying to make her feel good, have a bit of a laugh, compliment her, tell jokes. Look, other people do. Why are you picking on me?

'If she didn't like it, why didn't she ask me to stop? It's not as if she is a shrinking violet. She tells other people where to get off.

'Yeh, I rang her at home a couple of times. It's not against the law to ring a friend, is it? I just wanted a chat. Is she out to pillory me or something?

'She's overreacting. Behaving just like a women, saying 'no', but meaning 'yes', playing hard to get.

'She said if I wanted the tissues to come and get them. So I did. She knew damn well what we were talking about. She leaned back as I got behind the desk and I leant over and kissed her. She loved it.'

POINTS TO BE TAKEN FROM JANE'S INTERPRETATION:

• Andy's shouting and getting angry is unprofessional behaviour.

• Recipients of harassment do not ask for this treatment.

- Recipients are not responsible for asking the harasser to stop.

- All employees should know what is acceptable and professional conduct for the workplace.

- What Andy did may well have been unlawful. Sexual harassment may constitute sex discrimination and is unlawful under the Sex Discrimination Act (1975).

- Jane should have known there was a sexual harassment policy in the company. Mr Hedges or someone should have talked to her when she was first employed about the organizations' sexual harassment policy and grievance procedure.

- If you ignore sexual harassment it will probably get worse.

- Jane is a new employee, a young graduate and this is her first job. Managers need to be aware that people like Jane are among the most vulnerable people in the workplace.

- Jane has a perfectly reasonable explanation for the tissue episode.

POINTS TO BE TAKEN FROM ANDY'S INTERPRETATION:

- Sexual harassment is determined by the person receiving it.

- What does he mean 'like an old married couple' and the 'odd fight', and 'kiss and make up'? Ask him to explain.

- Remember this is the workplace, not home, and professional behaviour is a requirement of all staff.

- Sexual harassment is not personal stuff. It is the role of the managers to prevent it from happening in the first place and to resolve it as soon as possible if it does happen.

- Andy is not denying that this has taken place. Rather, he is denying that it has had a negative effect on Jane.

- Andy should not have behaved like this in the first place and it certainly is not fair to put Jane in this insidious position.

- Andy is making assumptions about their relationship. He thinks they are friends.

- Did he check with her that she didn't mind being 'phoned at home in the evening?

- Jane is not overreacting. Andy has been misreading the signs for months. He needs to reassess how he treats colleagues, and especially women colleagues. He also needs some education about the 'No means No' campaign.

- Andy obviously likes sexual innuendoes.

CHAPTER TWELVE

Challenging the Harasser

Introduction

Whilst it is important to have policies in the workplace it is also good to empower employees themselves to stop the harassment at source. Because sexual harassment often happens on a one-to-one basis this is an important strategy for individuals to use if they feel confident enough.

This chapter looks at some practical ways of dealing with those who perpetrate sexual harassment. Not only will I describe some of the strategies I have used on sexual harassers myself, but there will also be examples of how other women have fought back. Although, of course, the best method to use in a particular case cannot be prescribed, there is a range of different ways of thinking about what to do. One of the first things for a recipient to do is to think clearly about the options available and then for her to plan her actions with care.

What are you up against?

Sexual harassers come in all shapes and sizes, old, young, short, fat, bald, black, white, blonde, married, single, divorced and separated. They occupy a variety of positions, and might be the managing director, the chair of the board, the caretaker who calls the female staff 'dear' or 'love', or the younger men who think it amusing to display page three openly on their desks. Nor is there only a particular type of woman harassed. Sexual harassment affects many women in many different situations, irrespective of the clothes they wear, their actions, behaviour, looks or age. Dealing with a man who sexually harasses you is particularly difficult when there is a need to retain a professional relationship with him and when he is in a position of power. Thus, the male manager who calls the female staff 'ladies' and treats them in a patronizing way is often more difficult to confront than a colleague who tells sexist jokes. Often one of the problems with confronting someone like a male manager is that the behaviour may have been going on for some time, even years, others haven't complained, and now you have decided to take a stand.

Dealing with sexual harassment

There are basically three major ways of dealing with incidents of sexual harassment: via the organization's harassment policy and grievance procedures; by taking control yourself and challenging the perpetrator; or by remaining silent. Which one you should choose will be dependent on a number of variables: the relationship of the perpetrator to you; the circumstances in which it occurs; your feelings; the actual nature of the harassment; your role in the organization; whether you work in a team or by yourself, and the likely outcomes. A further factor concerns the organization in which you study or work, and whether it has the necessary machinery to cope with a complaint.

Doing it yourself

This section looks at the various options you have, as a recipient of harassment. I shall discuss the ways in which you can deal with it yourself, or ask a friend to help you deal with it informally, or how as a group you can act together to stop offensive behaviour. Remember, though, whom you confide in or ask to help may have a bearing on what happens. In some organizations, managers have a responsibility to ensure that no discrimination occurs. To tell someone who is obliged to act may result in the complaint automatically becoming a formal incident.

Whether you feel you can deal with the harasser on your own or you need help will depend on whether he is in a position of authority over you, a colleague or a subordinate. In some cases gathering the courage to do it yourself is the best option, because the incident remains private, less embarrassment is caused and the likelihood of the harasser and you re-establishing a working relationship is higher if you are the only people who know about it. Many men are unaware of how intrusive or patronizing their behaviour can be and it only takes a person to point out its inappropriateness of this for them to stop.

Of course, you may not want to keep it entirely as a private matter and would wish to make a formal complaint through your line manager (assuming she or he is not the perpetrator), and this is your choice. (For this course of action see the next section.)

Sexual harassment is exacerbated by the gender-role stereotyping which influences how women and men believe they should behave and what behaviours are regarded by some people as being 'normal' or 'natural'. However, irrespective of how others view certain behaviour, as we have seen in Chapter 2: Defining Sexual Harassment, the recipient of the actions must determine whether she found them welcome or not.

Some men believe that it is their duty to take care of women and girls, because of the myth that women and girls need looking after. This explains the often paternalistic or 'macho' ways of behaving of some men. Three simple examples are the opening of doors for women, insisting on always walking on the road side of the pavement and ushering women into rooms first. These are all traces of men's and women's learned social behaviours and have been regarded for many years as 'good manners'. Whilst some of these traditional behaviours are disappearing, as women open doors, walk on the outside and invite men to walk into rooms first, the beliefs about men and women's roles in society are still deeply entrenched. One of the most obvious forms of male patronage is the use of terms like 'dear', 'love' and 'petal'. To many men (and some women too) these are not patronizing names or anything to get upset about, for the intention is to make women feel comfortable and wanted, and to challenge this mode of speaking would be taken by some men to be churlish.

Before challenging sexual harassers it is important, therefore, that you are aware of the possible ramifications. As I have said, some men are keen to know how their behaviour offends and take seriously what you say to them. Others may not be so understanding and may well become extremely angry, verbally abusive or even violent, or use their rank to apply further detriment at a later stage.

I once received a postcard of a particularly unpleasant nature from a lecturer in the university at which I was a student. This arrived immediately before an exam I was about to have, of which he was to be the major examiner. I wrestled with the issue of confronting him before the examination and risking failing, or of waiting until afterwards, when, if I had failed, he may have seen my challenge as one of 'sour grapes'.

I decided on the former strategy and went to see him. He was busy and offered to come to my study as soon as he was free. When he arrived and I told him that I had found the postcard unacceptable, embarrassing, intimidating and sexually suggestive, he became extremely angry, abusive, insulting and loud. At one point I was scared that he would act violently. I had not assessed the situation very wisely. Confrontations in a private space, such as a study or office, are not particularly safe, as you may not be able to judge how the person will react.

Before you confront the perpetrator it might be wise to see one of the sexual harassment advisers in your organization. You could talk through with this person what you intend to do, when you intend to do it and to rehearse some of the things you might say. This course of action has the advantage that someone else is in the picture if the perpetrator does not stop and the harassment escalates. Any approach to an adviser should be confidential and before you do disclose what has happened to you it may be important to ask what the organization's policy is.

There are three ways of personally challenging a perpetrator: face to face, by letter and by phone. Each requires thought as to its appropriateness, safety and likelihood of success. I shall take each separately.

FACE-TO-FACE CONFRONTATION

When planning to tell the perpetrator that you find his behaviour offensive, rehearse your words, actions, and body language with a friend or in front of the mirror so that you do not get tongue-tied.

- Use direct eye contact.

- Speak clearly and slowly.

- State clearly the behaviour or comments which make you uncomfortable or angry and when they occurred.

- Concentrate on what you felt about the inappropriate behaviour, not on what he thought was intended.

- Do not undermine your complaint by smiling or apologizing.

- Do not be concerned about hurting the perpetrator's feelings or damaging his ego.

- Do not be put off by his attempt to dismiss, trivialize or belittle your experience.

- Remember you are not a passive helpless victim: you have the right to put your views.

- Remember you did not ask for it and you did not deserve it.

- Be clear about what you want to happen now (i.e. that the behaviour should stop, confidentiality be respected and that positive working relations resume).

- Once you have finished, turn and walk away. Do not engage in an argument about what he thought he was doing, or what he thinks of you and people like you.

The question of when to confront him is important. You could wait until the harassment happens again, having planned and practised a good response in the meantime, or you could decide on a particular time so that you are in control of the situation. Do not rush into the confrontation just because you see him approaching you down a corridor, unless you are well prepared. The sooner you confront him, on your terms, however, the better you will probably feel.

You will also need to consider where to do this; in his office, or workplace, or in more neutral territory such as the corridor or canteen. His office will offer you confidentiality because you will be the only two, but it does give him the opportunity to abuse you further. On the stairs or in the common room may offer you better protection from haranguing, by the presence of others.

A DRAFT LETTER TO A PERPETRATOR*

One way of confronting a perpetrator is to write him a letter explaining what he is doing that you do not like, how it is upsetting you, how it is affecting your work and what you want him to do about it. It is important that you tell him where and when the behaviour took place and what you heard him say, and what he did.

The letter is in four sections.

1) State the facts as you see them, in detail. Do not use euphemisms, emotive language or threats. For example:

> Dear Mr Brown,
>
> While I was working at the office photocopier around 2.30 pm on April 2nd, you walked past me, brushing up against my back as you passed, even though there was plenty of free walkspace in the area. At that time, you also remarked that 'I certainly knew how to push the right buttons'. A few minutes later, you returned to the photocopy area where I was continuing to work, and, standing between the machine and the table where I was sorting documents, looked me up and down and asked me to go out with you on Friday night. When I declined, you became quite insistent and said that you were tired of my 'hard-to-get-games' and that you 'knew' I wanted to go out with you. When I said I just wanted to be left alone to do my work, you angrily muttered that I was a 'prick teaser' and left. You have also asked me out on three other occasions and I have always declined.

2) Describe your feelings and any damages to study plans or career. For example:

> Such encounters with you leave me feeling confused and upset. I find myself avoiding situations where I'm likely to be alone in case you come by. My work is suffering as a result and I'm not as efficient and productive. It is also difficult for me to work in meetings with you.

3) Describe what you would like to happen now. For example:

> I want you to stop asking me to go out with you, making sexual comments and touching me. I want to be able to do my work without distractions and work with you on a purely professional basis.

---

* This letter first appeared in *Glamour Magazine*, August 1983. It was written by Dr Mary P Rowe, a consultant in sexual harassment and special assistant to the president of the Massachusetts Institute of Technology.

4) The letter should be signed and dated.

Keep a photocopy of the letter that is given to the harasser. You should deliver the letter in person and if possible have someone, possibly a sexual harassment adviser, witness the delivery. The presence of a witness will indicate to the harasser that his behaviour is known and further action may be taken if he continues the harassment. Make a note of the date and time you delivered the letter, the name of the witness and the response of the receiver.

A POSSIBLE 'PHONE CALL TO A PERPETRATOR

Another way of confronting a perpetrator is to 'phone him and explain to him that what he is doing to you is upsetting you, it is affecting your work and that you want this unwanted behaviour to stop. It is important that you tell him where and when the behaviour took place and what you heard him say, and what he did. You may wish to write a script for yourself so that you will not be put off. If he refuses to listen or won't let you speak, hang up. Do not engage in an argument on the 'phone. You may consider 'phoning him at home in the evening, if you think the presence of his wife will silence his retorts. The call is in four parts.

1) State the facts as you see them in detail. Do not use euphemisms, emotive language or threats. For example:

> Hello, is that Mr Green? It's Sue Jones here. I am ringing you because I wish to talk to you. Please do not interrupt me. The treatment you have been giving me over the past two months has been upsetting and embarrassing for me. There are two incidents that I want to remind you of.

> The first was in the canteen when you put a tray between my legs and said that you bet I wished that it was something else and the second time was when you came up to me when I was collating some materials and you patted me on the bottom.

2) Describe your feelings and any damages to study plans or career. For example:

> I have found each of these situations embarrassing and offensive. I am angry and upset by your behaviour. I am now avoiding places where I

know you will be and cannot concentrate on the work I have to do. I have been sick at the thought of coming to work and am distressed by your behaviour. I have been to the doctor and he says I am suffering from stress.

3) Describe what you would like to happen now. For example:

I want you to stop touching me and making sexual comments to me. I want to be able to do my work without distractions and work with you on a purely professional basis. I have discussed the situation with a sexual harassment adviser and she is aware that I have made this call. I do not want to take this matter any further and I want it to remain confidential. (Then ring off.)

Make a note of the date and time you made the 'phone call, inform the adviser of this and make a note of any response that is made by the harasser.

4) Keep a record of what you said to the harasser. By telling the perpetrator that you have sought advice from the sexual harassment adviser will indicate to him that his behaviour is known and further action may be taken if he continues the harassment.

Formal complaints

Formal complaints are those that are communicated to someone in authority in the organization in which you work. The complaint could be in the form of a written declaration to the manager, a complaint made to your union representative, a formal approach to a solicitor, or a case taken against the company for sex discrimination or constructive dismissal.

Formal written complaints have to be lodged with one of the people in an organization who has responsibility for acting on the complaint. In most organizations these are personnel managers, human resource managers, managing directors or executive officers. Once you have lodged a formal complaint (see Chapter 7: A Grievance Procedure) it is the responsibility of that person to deal with the allegation swiftly, competently and fairly. You are justified in taking the case to an Industrial Tribunal if they fail to do so.

For example, a woman, Mrs Haines, contacted me one morning and told me that she felt she was being sexually harassed. The incident had happened that morning. She had arrived at work (the first day following her promotion to a senior management position) and was confronted by a male colleague with the rumour that she had only been given the position because she had slept with the managing director. She immediately went to the managing director with this rumour and asked for his help in dealing with it. His response was to laugh and feel somewhat flattered by the gossip. She rang me. I rang the Advisory Conciliation and Arbitration Service (ACAS) for help. Their advice was that she should ask the managing director again to deal with the case. If he was not able, or prepared, to sort it out, the woman should walk out of the position and claim constructive dismissal through an Industrial Tribunal. The ACAS conciliator advised me that she would have a strong case and would probably win.

When Mrs Haines confronted her boss with the action she would take if he refused to treat the incident seriously, he was immediately repentant. He called a meeting of all senior managers, scotched the rumour, talked about malicious gossip and threatened disciplinary action should the rumour continue. The incident was resolved.

The point of this example is that it is the responsibility of the manager to act, and to do so quickly, clearly and to good effect. Failure to do this could result in court action.

Seeking advice from your union representative will probably have similar results. As soon as a person in a position of authority knows of your complaint action should be taken at a formal level.

Confidentiality

Confidentiality should be maintained at all times and only those directly concerned – the perpetrator, any witnesses, the recipient, and the person with whom you lodge the complaint – should know the details of the incident. Whilst these people will be expected to maintain confidentiality, in my experience silence around such a case is extremely difficult to monitor and should not be relied upon. In every sexual harassment policy there should be a clause which discusses what action will be taken if the recipient is further victimized or the harassment is repeated. Victimization of a recipient of harassment, or of a witness of harassment who wishes to make a complaint, is unlawful.

Doing nothing

Doing nothing is a third possible strategy, and one you may prefer to use. That is ok. It is understandable that when women receive unwanted attention from males, whose behaviour is supported by individual, structural and cultural power within society, they remain quiet. One reason for keeping quiet is that much of this kind of male behaviour is condoned and sanctioned as 'normal' and 'natural', and the recipient may not identify it as sexual harassment or might believe nothing can be done about it. To make complaints is very difficult in a society where unwanted male attention is mislabelled as flattery. If a person does complain, her behaviour is often interpreted as her betraying a lack of sense of humour, or being a prig or a man-hater and as a consequence she may be ostracized from her social set.

If the harassment is of a jokey nature, as it often is in many organizations where men tell jokes about parts of a woman's body, or make sexist comments and innuendoes for a laugh, women often find it difficult to separate the negative feelings of embarrassment from the positive feelings of belonging to a group. For this reason they remain quiet. Some women not only remain quiet, they seem to be going along with it at the time, joking with men and laughing derogatorily at some aspect of femaleness. While for many there is a contradiction in what they feel about the behaviour and what they do about it, they believe that for the present, at least, it is better to remain silent.

Keeping quiet about sexual harassment, however, is not the preserve of shy women. Recently, a few days after a lecture I gave to a group of professional women and men, the organizer, a man well into his 60s whom I had met on three or four occasions, and who had been present at the talk (on sexual harassment), invited me to a formal lunch party where he made a public comment about no sexual harassment being allowed during the meal because of my presence. This publicity was surprising, embarrassing, and trivialized the whole issue. All the lunch guests smiled or laughed. On my departing, this man kissed me on the forehead. The frustrating point was that, even after my lecture, he had not only not understood the issues of sexual harassment, but had subsequently harassed *me*. And yet I said nothing about it. If I complained I might not be given more work for this organization.

But did I remain silent for financial or career reasons only? Of course, these are valid, but I think there are others. Women are not taught to be demanding. In fact, little girls are trained to be passive, to put up with discomfort and to please others, initially their fathers and brothers, then their husbands. One of the reasons that women find it hard to ask males to stop particular behaviour is that they think it might give offence. Women do not like to be assertive, especially towards men, as this behaviour is often considered rude. Consequently they are often more likely to put up with it, than confront.

Whilst remaining silent is one alternative to confrontation, its ramifications should also be considered. At an individual level, unless behaviour is challenged, it is unlikely to stop and may get worse. Alternatively, it may not get worse, but stay exactly the same, and what changes is your tolerance to it. A young woman who worked in a bank told me that her boss used to call her 'Jan Darling' whenever he spoke to her. At the beginning she thought this was polite and acceptable. As she got to know him better and, in particular, his attitudes and values towards women (he thought women should stay at home and look after the children), she began to dislike this form of address. She felt unable to ask him to stop because she had accepted it for all those months previously. Her level of distress over her boss's attitude to her and other women, symbolized by the words 'Jan Darling', finally forced her into applying for another job and leaving that branch.

At a more universal level, remaining quiet does nothing to promote change of all men's behaviour in a general way. If all women were able to challenge all men's unwanted attentions successfully, then men's behaviour would have to change. Perhaps it is because so many of us remain silent that no systematic and constant pressure is brought to bear. At one institution where I worked, a group of us made badges on which was written the slogan 'The Dear Hunters', as a protest against men calling us 'dear' and 'love'. Perhaps each institution should promote a week in which everyone is encouraged to 'Speak out about Sexual Harassment'.

Diaries

Even if you feel you are unable to do anything about the harassment, you can begin to keep a diary about the behaviour, noting down the time it happened, location, any witnesses, what he did/said, what you did/said and what others did/said. Also make a note of how this behaviour affected your work, studies or health. If you do decide to make a complaint, take the diary with you and show it to the person you are complaining to.

If you take time off work and go to the doctor suffering from stress-related illnesses, describe to her or him what is happening to you at work, and say that you are suffering from sexual harassment. Ask them to write it in your medical records. If the case were to come to an investigation or an Industrial Tribunal this could be useful evidence.

Collective responses

One of the common traits of sexual harassers is that they direct their behaviour to many women, not just one. In other words they are serial sexual harassers. It is patently clear that in these cases sexual harassment is not a manifestation of sexual interest in a particular woman. Some men who sexually harass women are not choosey about the recipient of their unwanted attentions. It has been found that often one man in the office or organization is responsible for harassment of several employees. Because of the difficulty of naming sexual harassment, because harassers usually harass secretively or when no one else is about, and because of society's response to sexual harassment, the recipient remains quiet about her feelings, thinking that she is the only one to be attracting this attention or else that others don't mind it, when in fact they do.

It is important, then, to talk about incidents of sexual harassment to other women in the institution. Name names, point out the harasser, and generally make it clear that you know what he is doing and others do too, and that his actions will no longer be tolerated. The chances are that if he is sexually harassing you he is also sexually harassing a number of other women too.

Of course there may well be a problem here. If you talk to other women who are not aware of the problem of sexual harassment and who have never thought about it as unwanted, embarrassing or intimidating, their response may well be one of disbelief or laughter at your concern over what to them is a trivial incident. Although this is difficult, there are two strategies that might help. Try to choose a person whom you think is aware. Alternatively you could try to explain to a friend what it is that is happening and what you feel, discussing the wider social implications of male dominance and female oppression and in this way try to raise her awareness at the same time.

Recently I was speaking to a woman about the work I do on sexual harassment and she told me that she went along with it, but only a certain way. 'After all', she said, 'people who object to wolf-whistles are really quite priggish. It doesn't do any harm, does it?'

In my opinion, wolf-whistles *are* harmful: they are intimidating, embarrassing, an invasion of one's space, an interruption and an insult. In effect, the man (or men) are letting you know that they think you are attractive. But do you want to know what strange men think about your body or your looks? What do they know about you? Do they know what you are like? Do they like your personality, your thoughts, your ideas and your sense of humour? Clearly not, because they don't know you. In effect, by means of a wolf-whistle they are giving your body, or parts of it, a mark out of ten and letting you know that they think you are attractive, sexy, or just worth annoying. In other words, you are being treated as a sex object.

One strategy used by a group of secretaries working in a large government office to combat the unwanted attentions of a sexual harasser was to make his name public, without letting anyone know who they were. In casual conversations a number of the women employees found that one of their senior managers, a 55-year old man, was harassing them all in a variety of ways. He made comments about their appearances such as, 'I do like it when you wear leather'; 'That little number you were wearing yesterday was really pretty.' He made sexual innuendoes too. One of the secretaries described an incident when she went into his office to confirm an appointment. She said to him, 'Mr Western, Mrs Ash has rung and confirmed the appointment for tomorrow. She is coming at 12 o'clock, is that ok?' Mr Western, with a leering grin on his face replied, 'I don't mind what time Mrs Ash comes, I just like it when they come.'

Further behaviour from Mr Western included unwanted touching, stroking, patting and sexist and sexual jokes. After sharing many of their experiences with each other the women secretaries decided to act collectively. After work one night they went into the men's loos and wrote with their lipstick on the mirror, 'John Western sexually harasses secretaries'. In the morning there was apparently a stunned silence from the men as each made a visit to the lavatory and found the accusation. John Western modified his behaviour.

The discussion of incidents of sexual harassment among women in the same work institution helps to build collective strength. If a woman knows that she is not alone, that this treatment is not unique to her and the harassment is generally, not specifically, directed towards her, she is likely to become more confident about dealing with it, either alone or with others. In a group of women, strategies can be brain-stormed and the most appropriate one selected to put into practice, taking account of the particular harasser, his *modus operandi* and the institution in which it is occurring.

Union representation

One possible strategy to use, if you are a recipient of sexual harassment, is to contact your union. Most unions take the matter of sexual harassment seriously. They have policies which make explicit their views on sexual harassment and which give advice on what to do.

Whilst informal proceedings are recommended so that a complaint can be resolved quickly, this is not always possible and formal proceedings are then needed. At this stage it will be necessary to contact your representative, the local negotiating secretary, an officer of your local association, the Executive member for your area or your Regional Official. They will be able to give you appropriate advice and support on what action to take.

Test out your assertiveness

Below are some test cases. Practise your confrontation skills:

- Every morning as you come into the office the lift operator calls you 'love' and if you are the only person in the lift makes some sexist comment or innuendo. Once he told you that he liked what you were wearing, especially the two bumps on the front.

  One morning you decide to confront him. What do you say?

- You are a tele-sales operator. You have a boss whom you rarely see because he works in the Head Office and you work locally. However, whenever you and he have to speak on the 'phone together he makes some kind of suggestive remark. Sometimes it's to do with what you did at the weekend, why you must be tired or what he could do to make your sex life great again. You have ignored them up until now. One morning when you ring him to give him some information that he wants, he asks you how you are. You

116

tell him that you have a sore throat. He replies: 'I have a brilliant cure for sore throats'. You say, 'Oh, what is it?' He says, 'Oral sex'.

You decide to confront him. Do you wait until he next comes to the office or will you challenge him over the phone? What do you say?

- One of the clerks in your office buys the Sun every morning and brings it to work. At the coffee break which he has in the office he always turns to page three and starts making comments about the shape of the women's breasts. You usually take no notice.

One day you decide to confront him. What do you say to him? Where and when do you challenge his behaviour?

- While you are taking notes for your supervisor one morning he deliberately pushes up against you and rubs his crotch into your knee. He looks at you while he does so, daring you to say something. You do nothing at the time, but you are very upset, angry and embarrassed. You think about it and talk it over with a colleague.

You decide to challenge him. What do you say?

CHAPTER THIRTEEN

Taking a Case to an Industrial Tribunal

Clive Gillott BA, FIPM, Employment Law Consultant

Introduction

This chapter concentrates on the processes involved in taking a case to an Industrial Tribunal. It considers the grounds necessary, how to make a claim and other relevant factors in relation to the Industrial Tribunal. It is written from the perspective of believing you have been harassed and either taking a case yourself or seeking help to present it.

On what grounds can you make a claim?

There are two grounds on which an application to an Industrial Tribunal can be made:

   a) **sex discrimination**

   b) **constructive dismissal.**

a) Sex discrimination

If you are an employee who has been sexually harassed at work by a man employed by the same employer you may be able to bring a claim to an Industrial Tribunal.

There are two ways to make a claim. First of all, you can claim that this male employee unlawfully discriminated against you on the grounds of your sex when he treated you less favourably than he treats or would treat a man, and that this was to your detriment. Detriment means a disadvantage and certainly includes loss of opportunity, e.g. transfer, promotion, overtime, and loss of employment. Detriment can also include offensive acts about which a reasonable employee could complain because it adversely affected her working environment.

Your claim would not only be against the male employee but also against your employer when there is a separate body, e.g. a company, a local authority, a voluntary organization.

b) Constructive dismissal

The second way into a Tribunal is to resign, with or without giving notice, because your employer's conduct is intolerable to you. In law this is regarded as dismissal even though you left the job, and is referred to as *constructive dismissal*. You may be able to claim both sex discrimination and constructive dismissal, but if you are successful you will receive only one amount of compensation.

An Industrial Tribunal will want to know whether the employer's conduct was a significant breach going to the root of the contract of employment, or whether it showed that the employer no longer intended to be bound by one or more of the essential terms of the contract.

Sexual harassment can give rise to a claim of constructive dismissal because it may involve a breach of what is called *an implied term of the contract*, namely that an employer will not without reasonable and proper cause, conduct himself in a manner calculated or likely to destroy or seriously damage the relationship of trust and confidence between the employer and the employee.

A breach of this implied term could arise either from a single serious act of sexual harassment by a male employee, or from a series of acts, whether serious or not. If the claim arises from a series of acts, you can resign after the last one, when you in effect say, 'enough is enough'. This is known as the 'last straw' argument.

A finding by a Tribunal that there has been a constructive dismissal does not mean it is automatically unfair. The fairness of the dismissal is a separate decision, but one would expect it to be found unfair.

Tribunals expect employees to resign without delay if they think there has been a fundamental breach (as defined above). Otherwise Tribunals may well decide that the employee has decided the breach is not so serious and has lost her right to claim constructive dismissal. One way to keep the right open is to make clear in writing that the act complained of is intolerable and that resignation is withheld pending a satisfactory outcome. This position should not be held indefinitely.

It should be borne in mind that if an employer treats you less favourably than he would treat a man because you have made a claim of sex discrimination, then he has unlawfully victimized you, and this is a ground for an additional complaint to the Tribunal.

Who can make a claim?

a) Sex discrimination

There are no age limits, or minimum service or minimum hour requirements necessary to make a claim. You must be able to show that you are an employee, i.e., subject to some control by the employer, not working on your own account, paying income tax and national insurance.

b) Constructive dismissal

You must be below the normal age of retirement and you must have been continuously employed by your employer either:

- for at least two years, with normal working hours of at least 16 a week; or

- for at least five years, with normal working hours of at least eight a week and less than 16.

Invoking the grievance procedure

You should not make a claim to an Industrial Tribunal, on any grounds, until you are sure it is the most appropriate step for you to take.

Certainly, for less serious acts of sexual harassment you should attempt to stop the harassment by the harasser yourself (see Chapter 12: Challenging the Harasser), talk the case through with a sexual harassment adviser (see Chapter 10: Your Role as an Adviser) or complain to someone in a position of authority before deciding to take a case to an Industrial Tribunal. You should then allow a reasonable time to have your complaint investigated. If your complaint is found justified, you can expect some action to be taken to prevent repetition of the offensive conduct.

Many employers have formal grievance procedures and you should follow yours. Some might even have specific harassment procedures. The reason for this advice is that it may well cure the problem, and it is likely to weaken your case at the Tribunal if you have not given your employer a chance to consider it.

Furthermore, if you have complained formally, and your employer fails to investigate adequately, and fails to take reasonable steps to protect you, your case will be considerably strengthened because a failure to investigate properly can in itself be discriminatory.

Similarly, in a claim of constructive dismissal, the case can be weakened by the failure to seek an internal resolution of your complaint.

On the other hand, a gross act of sexual harassment could leave you with no option but to walk out immediately, particularly if it was committed by the most senior person in a small business.

There is nothing to stop you registering your claim with the Tribunal, at the same time as making it clear that you do not want the claim to be heard until your internal complaint is resolved satisfactorily. The claim can be subsequently withdrawn or amended.

Time limits for making a claim

a) Sex discrimination

A claim must normally be received at the Central Office of Industrial Tribunals (COIT), 100 Southgate Street, Bury St Edmunds, Suffolk, IP33 2AQ, Tel: (0284) 762300, within three months beginning with the date of the final act complained of. The form to use is an Industrial Tribunal No. 1 (IT1). (Note that this means three calendar months, therefore a period beginning with 30 November ends on 28th February. Moreover, if the act complained of occurred on 10th March, the closing date would be the 9th June. And if the 9th June is a Saturday of Sunday, the closing date is Friday 7th or 8th June.)

b) Constructive dismissal

The time limit is the same except that it is measured from the date employment ended.

If you really cannot meet the deadline with the Industrial Tribunal, send in a letter to COIT stating that you are making a claim of sex discrimination and/or constructive dismissal against your employer (named) and that you will submit the Industrial Tribunal form in the near future.

Keeping your papers and information in order

No doubt you will have collected several documents already; letters, notes of meetings, and documents relating to your employment. There will certainly be more documents, and you will need to keep them all together so that you can refer to them if necessary. They need to be kept in date order, and you may find it useful to have two files, one on administrative matters and one on the substance of the case. Ring-binders or wallets are best for holding them.

Keep a diary of what has happened and what should happen on future dates. Make a note of telephone calls and conversations. Later it will be necessary to extract from all this the evidence to be presented to the Tribunal, if it takes place.

Sources of help

You may feel quite confident about submitting the IT1 and the Questions Procedure Form (see below), and handling your case after that entirely on your own. No one will hold that against you. On the contrary, you will be applauded.

However, not everyone is so confident and it is normally useful to have someone else who is not emotionally involved to act as your representative, or at least to advise you on the merits of your case and the best way to present it.

The Equal Opportunities Commission can provide a solicitor to present your case, but it cannot afford to support every applicant in this way. It can also provide advice and information booklets.

There is a specific organization to deal with cases of sexual harassment. It is called Women against Sexual Harassment (WASH) and they can offer experience, help and advice. They can be contacted at the following address: 312 The Chandlery, 50 Westminster Bridge Road, London SE1 7QY, Tel: (071) 721 7592.

If you belong to a trade union, you may be entitled to its support for a case with a good prospect of success. Free advice, and possible representation, is available from the Citizens Advice Bureaux, but they have limited resources. You could go to a private solicitor but you would have to pay for her or his time in preparation, representation and any follow-up. This could be very expensive and the solicitor would want to be sure of your ability to pay. Legal aid is available only for those on very low incomes, and even then is restricted to advice, without representation. There are insurance companies that include legal support for employment claims as part of policies for other purposes, e.g. House Contents Insurance. They will only support cases with a reasonable prospect of success.

Finally, there are private consultants who will provide advice and representation, and require a fee only if the case is won or settled out of court. They require a percentage of the amount gained. They also will support only cases with a reasonable prospect of success.

Starting the claim procedure

To create the 'originating application', as it is called, you need to fill in a form numbered IT1. A form can be obtained from any Job Centre or branch of the Citizens Advice Bureaux.

Filling it in is reasonably straightforward, but if there is anything you do not know, or are unsure about when answering the questions of fact, you can always supply the information later. Handwriting is acceptable, but be as neat as possible,

What is most important to complete is the answer to question 10 – full details of your complaint. Your adviser, if you have one, can be helpful here. You can continue on a separate sheet if there is not enough space, or you can write in the space, *'Please see attached sheet'* and put all the details on a separate sheet. Remember to sign and date the attachment, and keep a copy to add to your file. The details of your complaint do not need to include everything that was said or done, but should say enough to make clear what and who you are complaining about. Make clear what act or acts you consider were discriminatory, or caused you to resign.

You may have some documents, such as letters or notes of meetings. You can refer to these if necessary when completing the IT1, but *do not* send them with the IT1.

Post the IT1 to the Central Office of Industrial Tribunals in Bury St Edmunds in good time to beat the deadline (see above for full address).

Questions Procedure Form

In addition it is recommended that you also get a Questions Procedure Form. These are available from the Equal Opportunities Commission, Quay Street, Manchester M3 3HN, Tel: (061) 833 9244. The questions have been devised to encourage the employer to describe in more detail his or her company's attitude to issues of equal opportunity and to find out pertinent information about relevant policies and the implementation of them.

You can send this to your employer before the IT1 is submitted, but not later than 21 days after the IT1 is received by COIT.

The questionnaire can be used to require the employer to answer specific questions. There could be four outcomes:

i) You may conclude that you were not treated less favourably and may decide to drop the case. If you have already sent in the IT1 you must write to COIT requesting that the case be abandoned.

ii) Your employer may agree that there has been discrimination and resolve the matter with you outside the tribunal process.

iii) The replies may confirm your wish to take the case forward. The replies can be used in evidence.

iv) The employer may fail to reply to all or any of the questions. This may be seen by the Tribunal as further evidence of discrimination.

The Equal Opportunities Commission also provides some additional questions which you can use. However, the onus is on you to ask only questions which produce answers that are helpful to your case or harmful to your employer's case.

The employer's response

COIT send your IT1 to the appropriate Regional Office of Industrial Tribunals (ROIT), which is usually the region in which your employment is located. Most regions have local tribunals to which your case can be referred ultimately. The ROIT sends your IT1 to the respondent, that is the employer you have named. You are known as the applicant.

The respondent then has 14 days from receipt of the IT1 to submit their *'Notice of Appearance'* on form IT3. Quite often the respondent requests an extension of time and this is usually granted .

Maybe after four to six weeks you will receive from ROIT a copy of the respondent's reply. You can expect a denial of your claim, even though it may be soundly based. Few employers will readily admit that discrimination has occurred.

However, they may be willing to settle out of court, for convenience, or to avoid adverse publicity or because they know, but will not admit, they have a weak case.

ROIT automatically sends the Advisory, Conciliation and Arbitration Service (ACAS) copies of the IT1 and IT3. ACAS will appoint an officer to deal with your case. He or she will be able to discuss various aspects of the case. ACAS have a statutory duty as an independent body to try to achieve a conciliated settlement, agreed by both parties. Either side, or ACAS, may initiate the process. The settlement, if achieved, is for a sum of money, by definition less than could be awarded by the Industrial Tribunal, and sometimes related to the provision of satisfactory references.

The agreed amount is in full and final settlement of the claim. It is called a COT 3 settlement, because that is the number of the form used. The case is therefore withdrawn.

Further particulars, discovery and witness orders

If the case is proceeding to a Tribunal hearing either side may seek more information *(further particulars)* or more documents *(discovery or disclosure)*, from the other side.

In a sex discrimination case, the Question Procedures Form from the EOC is likely to serve these purposes, since both information and documents can be requested.

However, if one side is unwilling to co-operate in this process, the other side can apply to the Tribunal, in advance of the hearing, for an order on the first side to produce the information and/or documents. The Tribunal will want to know what is needed, why it is needed and why it is refused. They will decide according to their view of what the parties need to enable justice to be done, and to save costs.

Similarly, the Tribunal may be willing to order a reluctant witness to appear on behalf of the party requesting the witness.

Preparing for the Industrial Tribunal

Eventually, after consultation with both sides, a date will be fixed for the hearing. It is your job, or your representative's if you have one, to advise your witnesses, if you have any, and to prepare all the documentary evidence that you will refer to. This is known as *'the bundle'*. The respondent does the same, and both sides are requested (required) to exchange their bundles well in advance of the hearing.

Once the date is fixed it will not be changed at the request of either party unless there are exceptional circumstances.

Note that attempts at settlement can go on right up to the hearing, and indeed until just before a decision is announced. Sometimes the Chairperson will obliquely, or even directly, suggest the parties try to settle, even after hearing the evidence (or at least some if it).

In preparing for the Tribunal, you or your representative will need to remember the following:

1. It is for the applicant who complains of discrimination to make out her case. Thus if the applicant does not prove the case, on the balance of probabilities she will fail.

2. It is important to bear in mind that it is unusual to find direct evidence of discrimination. Few employers will be prepared to admit to discrimination.

3. The outcome of the case will therefore usually depend on what inferences it is proper to draw from the primary facts found by the Tribunal.

4. A finding of discrimination and a finding of a difference in sex will often point to the possibility of sex discrimination. In such circumstances the Tribunal will look to the employer for an explanation. If no explanation is put forward or if the Tribunal considers the explanation to be inadequate or unsatisfactory, it will be legitimate for the Tribunal to infer the discrimination was on the grounds of sex.

You should also remember that the employer's defence that he did not intend to discriminate will carry no weight. The Tribunal will consider the effects of his action on the person harassed.

What happens at the hearing?

If you are claiming sex discrimination, the Tribunal will require you to present your case first, setting out the facts as you know them. It is at this stage that you will derive most benefit from having a representative. What follows assumes that both sides are represented.

Your representative will begin by presenting a copy of your 'bundle' to each of the three persons on the Tribunal. The middle one is the Chairperson, who is legally qualified, and the other two are lay persons, one from the employer's panel, and one from the employee's representative's panel. One of these is likely to be a woman because it is a sex discrimination case, but it is not always possible.

Your representative will call you as the first witness, and you are required to take an oath or affirm. You representative will then take you through your evidence, introducing relevant documents along the way. This is known as *evidence-in-chief.* Your evidence is oral, but you may refer to your own notes made at the time that events occurred.

Once you have finished your evidence-in-chief, your employer's representative will cross-examine you. This is likely to be uncomfortable for you since her or his job is to try and cast doubt on the facts or interpretations you have given, and to begin to present the employer's case by registering disagreement with points in your case. It may also cause you distress to be reminded of the events that led to your claim.

After cross-examination has finished, the Tribunal may ask its questions first, and then allow your representative to re-examine you on points arising from the cross-examination or their examination; or it may reverse this order, or even allow two re-examinations.

The Chairperson may ask questions at any time, usually for clarification. The Chairperson has to take notes in longhand.

After your evidence is completed, your witness(es) will proceed in turn through exactly the same questioning. When all your witnesses are finished, the same process is adopted for the other side.

Your employer will then be asked to call his or her witnesses to give their evidence-in-chief. They will be cross-examined, and the value of an experienced representative on your side should be realized again.

Once all the evidence is presented, each side is allowed to sum up (preferably through representatives). The employer's side goes first and you have the last word. It is at this stage that references (not too many) may be made to case-law precedents that are relevant and helpful. Some discussion with the Chairperson may take place.

The Tribunal will then deliberate in private and announce its decision, time permitting. If they decide in your favour, it is necessary to consider compensation. If the decision is that there was sex discrimination the Tribunal will consider evidence and argument on injury to feelings and detriment or loss. If the decision is that there was no discrimination, but there was a constructive dismissal, compensation includes a basic award for loss of job and a compensatory award for continuing loss of earnings.

Compensation for constructive dismissal is limited by statute. Compensation for sex discrimination is not limited and can be considerably more, depending on the circumstances.

Self-representation

If you do decide to represent yourself at an Industrial Tribunal it is
suggested that you read the following texts:

- WASH Women Against Sexual Harassment: *Sexual Harassment of
  Women in the Workplace: A Guide to Legal Action*. 312 The
  Chandlery, 50 Westminster Bridge Road, London SE1 7QY, 1990.

- Robin Allen, *How to Prepare a Case for an Industrial Tribunal for
  Claims under the Sex Discrimination and Equal Pay Acts:* Equal
  Opportunities Commission, 1987.

- Michael Rubenstein, *Discrimination: A Guide to Relevant Case Law
  on Race and Sex Discrimination and Equal Pay,* Eclipse Group,
  London (undated).

CHAPTER FOURTEEN

Training and Professional Development

A day's programme

This chapter has been written to give an idea of what a day's training might look like. It describes suitable activities for a training day for people in your organization who are in managerial positions and who need to understand their role in countering sexual harassment.

The programme laid out in timed sessions below is followed by a description of the day's proceedings. It has been written largely in note form, signposting the salient points which the course leader will need to emphasize. Clearly each trainer will want to bring their own style, experiences and training tactics to the day. This is not a blueprint for action, rather a method for organizing training on sexual harassment.

Overheads and handouts will need to be made. For more information consult the training pack developed in conjunction with this book, *Countering Sexual Harassment* (Daniels Publishers, Cambridge).

The day would form part of a series of workshops and training days for the organization. Over a period of three months or so different groups of employees would be selected to attend a workshop on sexual harassment tailored to their needs. Thus women secretaries would need information about challenging and confronting a harasser; managers would need to discuss their role in the organization and how they can help prevent sexual harassment from happening. Workshops will also have to be arranged for people who are to be advisers to those who have been harassed.

A typical one day programme

The main aim of the training day is to raise managers' awareness of sexual harassment and to consider strategies, in terms of policies and practices, for dealing with this unwanted behaviour. To achieve these objectives we shall be looking at the relevant laws, exploring the misconceptions which mask the true impact of sexual harassment and addressing the questions which underlie this issue.

9.00	*Coffee and registration*
9.15	Introduction
9.25	Welcome: Setting the scene
9.45.	Activity One: Memories of harassment as a child
10.15	Activity Two: What is sexual harassment?
	Coffee
12.00	Activity Three: Why do the recipients of sexual harassment remain silent?
12.30	Activity Four: What are the consequences of sexual harassment
	• for the individual?
	• for the institution?
1.00	*Lunch*
1.45	Activity Five: Countering the myths and misconceptions of sexual harassment
2.30	Activity Six: A grievance procedure
3.00	*Tea*
3.15	Activity Seven: The role of the managers
3.45	Activity Eight: The anxious workplace
4.15	Activity Nine: Sexual harassment and the law
4.45	Questions and feedback
5.00	Close

The programme in detail

I shall attempt to describe the details of a day's training for a group of managers in one particular organization.

9.00: Coffee and registration

I begin each training with coffee, and give participants a copy of the programme if it hasn't been distributed beforehand.

9.15: Introduction

I think it is important, if at all possible to have a senior manager open the day's proceedings. This gives the day's participants the chance to hear from the managing director or senior executive that sexual harassment is an issue which is being taken seriously by this organization and that this group of people have their part to play in the countering of sexual harassment. The strength of opening in this way is that it gives validity to the training day. It shows that the management are taking it seriously.

9.25 Welcome: Setting the scene

There are four parts to your introduction: 1) Introducing yourself and the members of the group; 2) giving a health warning; 3) detailing the particular aims for the day; 4) giving a brief historical background to sexual harassment.

1) Introducing yourself and the group: Each person in the group introduces themselves. If the participants know each other there is no need for introductions but often, in a large company, this is not the case.

2) Health warning: In introducing the topic of sexual harassment I say something along these lines:

'This is not a comfortable topic. Sexual harassment confronts and challenges many behaviours which we take for granted or we have regarded as being "normal" or "natural". Some of you might get angry. There may be anger from some of you. I am going to ask you to keep hold of your temper and your cynical remarks if you feel this way. This day is not set up to point the finger at anyone, rather to raise the issues so that sexual harassment can be stopped. I would like to see this day as a time for learning and changing, not a battle ground.

'I am now going to speak directly to the women. (It is important that as trainers we do not use words that are patronizing or demeaning, so I always use the word "women" when talking about women and "men" when talking about men.)

'Today may bring up memories of times when you have been sexually harassed, even if you haven't called it this before. It may be painful, and you may feel very sad, or very angry. If you feel you want to leave, please do. I will be here during the breaks if you want to speak to me about anything then, but you can always contact me later. If you do leave I suggest you go home and call a friend, your partner, or someone who will understand what has happened and will support you. But please deal with it. Don't keep it quiet anymore.

'If, on the other hand, you wish to talk about it in front of the people here, either in a small group, or as a whole group, I hope the rest of the participants will treat you with care and consideration. I also want to mention confidentiality. During the course of the day some of you may hear about people who are victims or people who are harassers. Please do not take these stories out of this room'.

3) *Particular aims for the day*: In this section you will be detailing the overall aims for the day, whetting the participants' appetites and predicting forthcoming attractions. It is important that the participants have an understanding right at the outset of the kinds of things they can expect, as well as clear guidelines on what it is they need to learn from the day. Telling learners what they will be learning is sound educational practice. They will be off to a flying start if they know what is required of them. Never leave learners in the dark about what you want them to get out of a particular session. A list of aims could include:

• to become aware of the breadth and depth of sexual harassment (see Chapter 4: Statistics)

• to understand how difficult this topic is to discuss (see Chapter 2: Defining Sexual Harassment)

- to understand how 'normal' this behaviour is seen to be, how it is often identified by society as being part of, or conforming to, the required male image, and therefore how difficult it is to change (see Chapter 2: Defining Sexual Harassment)

- to understand the consequences of harassment for individuals and organizations (see Chapter 5: Consequences and Legal Implications)

- to understand how harassers often regard their behaviour as 'only being friendly' and the effect this has (see Chapter 2: Defining Sexual Harassment)

- to understand the power relation (see Chapter 3: The Power Dimension)

- to try and halt the continuation of harassment through education and awareness and to empower recipients (see Chapter 9: Countering Myths and Misconceptions)

- to be able to intervene and stop the harasser and get them to think about how their behaviour might be offensive (see Chapter 11: The Role of Management)

- to accept that sexual harassment is learned social behaviour. It is not inherent (see Chapter 2: Defining Sexual Harassment)

- to see how the law protects employees and how employers will always be liable for harassment of which they were informed but which they ignored

- to inform employers that they may be vicariously liable (even if unaware of the harassment), if an employee is shown to be guilty of sexual harassment during the course of their employment

- to find strategies to prevent rather than cure.

4) *Historical background to sexual harassment* (see Chapter 1: Putting Sexual Harassment in Context).

9.45. Activity One: Memories of harassment as a child

Organization: Have the participants make groups of three and describe and discuss an incident of bullying or unwanted behaviour that they remember happening when they were of school age. It may have been in a class, in the playground, at home, in the neighbourhood, and the antagonist may have been a friend, a relative. a teacher, a sibling or a stranger acting alone or in a group.

Time: Allow ten minutes for participants in their small groups to discuss the following questions:

• What did you feel at the time?

• How did it affect your behaviour?

• How did you deal with it at the time?

Aims: The aim of this session is to acknowledge and typify unwanted attention experienced by everyone and to make it real for each participant. The feelings underlying unwanted attention of any kind are very similar to those that recipients of sexual harassment experience. By identifying similar experiences in their own past, managers can be made aware of the importance of taking the matter seriously.

Plenary: At the end of the time ask them to return to the large group. Ask them to tell you what they talked about in their small groups and collate all their answers on a flip chart. I use the headings: Feelings, Behaviour, Action.

Expected outcomes:

• Feelings: Anger, frustration, fear, isolation, helplessness, guilt, loneliness, unhappiness, why me?, depression. *These are all fears which are also associated with being sexually harassed.*

• Behaviour: Avoiding certain areas, people, lessons, changing one's patterns, becoming quieter, more isolated, trying not to be noticed. Got up and did something about it. All *these are typical behaviours of sexually harassed people.*

- Action: Didn't do anything, didn't tell parents, remained silent, told someone and it got worse, told and it did get better. *Most of the responses here are to do with inaction, although sometimes there is a person who did do something and it was resolved. The main point is that most people who are sexually harassed do nothing because of fear and guilt.*

10.15 Activity Two: What is sexual harassment?

Organization: This session continues until 12.00 noon. During this time I take a coffee break when there seems to be a need, rather than interrupt a discussion for the sake of a timetable. Have the participants make new groups of three and ask them to discuss the term 'sexual harassment', bringing in their own experiences or cases they know about. Ask the groups to write down some sentences about sexual harassment with which they all agree. Some useful focusing activities are: Describe sexual harassment, how it happens, what it looks/feels like.

Time: This is quite a difficult activity. But is also extremely useful as it approaches people's own attitudes towards sexual harassment, recipients, perpetrators, what should be done, and who has the right to define it. I usually allow about 25–30 minutes for them to discuss the definition, then a further 30 minutes for each group to present back. Lastly I need 15 minutes to draw it all together and allow for other issues and concerns to be discussed.

Aims: This activity encourages participants to come to grips with the concept of sexual harassment, to widen their probably fairly narrow definition and to realize how difficult a subject it is to name and label.

Plenary: Re-form the participants as one group, and ask them to read out the statements on which they all agreed. I usually have this as a fairly informal session, people contributing to the development and refinement of the question, 'What is sexual harassment?' in whatever format is applicable. They are not expected to know all the answers and should be encouraged to say if they are not sure in a particular case. Another tack I use if I find a query difficult, is to throw it open to the group and say; 'That's an interesting question.

What do others think?' Remember the point of the day is education and changing attitudes through debate and discussion, not an examination of the facilitator's knowledge. Working things out as a group is a good way of sharing information, encouraging people to talk and getting to an answer by working on it, rather than giving definitive replies. Also, it is important to remember that every case of sexual harassment is different and there is no one right way to treat any case.

Expected outcomes: During the course of this session you will need to pull out the main points and focus on them and their centrality to sexual harassment. The points to be made are:

- Who decides what sexual harassment is? It is the recipient of harassment who decides what makes her feel uncomfortable and what is unwanted.

- Intention: What the perpetrator thought he was doing is irrelevant. The behaviour constitutes sexual harassment if the recipient finds it embarrassing, humiliating and/or threatening.

- Context: The context is extremely important. Who the harasser is – boss, co-worker or someone junior to the recipient – will have an effect on how she feels/handles the incident/acts. The what and the where are also important. If the place where she is harassed is isolated and dangerous, and she is alone, this might make the sexual harassment worse for her. Lastly, some actions, like a hug, are sometimes harassing and sometimes not. For example, we like hugs from the right person at the right time and in the right way. But it is also easy to experience a hug that is too huggy, too clingy, too stroky, leaving us feeling pawed, unwashed and embarrassed.

- Behaviours: Types of behaviour which can be harassing. Broadly these fall into categories of touching, verbal and non-verbal, gesturing and literary.

- Direct and indirect sexual harassment (see Chapter 2: Defining Sexual Harassment).

Coffee whenever it is needed.

12.00 Activity Three: Why do recipients of sexual harassment remain silent?

Organization: Again, get the participants into small groups and ask them to discuss the question: Why do recipients of sexual harassment remain silent?

Time: Approximately 15 minutes for group work and 15 minutes for plenary.

Aims: Here the particular aim is to have the participants focus on the difficulties surrounding sexual harassment and why recipients prefer to keep silent or hand in their notice, rather than make a complaint, or ask the perpetrator to stop. Have them reflect on the first session and the feelings associated with being bullied, to get at the heart of why recipients remain silent. Challenge the attitude, 'They should have complained; they could have done something, rather than just put up with it', and keep referring them to those feelings of fear, guilt and embarrassment. Also challenge the myth that many women make up incidents of sexual harassment. Whilst we have to acknowledge that a woman may lie about sexual harassment, I have never dealt with a case such as this. A woman is more likely to remain silent because of the embarrassment, fear and humiliation than talk about a subject she finds embarrassing, threatening, humiliating and distasteful. The much more difficult question to find an answer to is: How can a business develop and promote an ethos in which a recipient of sexual harassment feels entirely safe and confident to make a report? This activity will also lay the ground rules and begin to build up the necessary and appropriate attitudes managers need to display when dealing with a case of sexual harassment. They need to understand how important it is to be sensitive and open to a claim of harassment because of the power dimensions, the silence that surrounds it and recipient's feelings of guilt, depression and powerlessness.

Plenary: After the groups have been discussing for about ten minutes, I again use a flip chart to collate the whole group's answers.

Expected outcomes: The kinds of responses you will get to the question, 'Why do recipients remain silent?' will be:

- guilt,

- fear of losing one's job,

- fear of being thought difficult/prudish/having no sense of humour,

- believing you may have brought it on yourself,

- thinking no one will believe you, because he is the boss/a respected person/a nice man/a family man, etc.,

- the others in the office may think you are peculiar, others seem to laugh when he does similar things,

- you are the only person it has happened to,

- if you keep quiet he will probably stop,

- it will only get worse if you complain.

12.30 Activity Four: What are the consequences of sexual harassment for the individual and for the organization?

Organization: In small groups of three have the managers brainstorm what the consequences are for the individuals and the organization if nothing is done.

Four useful questions are:

- What are the short-term consequences for recipients of harassment?

- What are the short-term consequences for the organization?

- What are the long-term consequences for recipients of harassment?

- What are the long-term consequences for the organization?

Time: Approximately 15 minutes for group work and 15 minutes for plenary.

Aims: These questions are aimed at getting the managers to understand that sexual harassment is not a minor disruption for a few minutes, but that it can have severe consequences, both physically and psychologically, for the recipients. Whilst I prefer to concentrate on the consequences for the recipients in the short and long term, there are also consequences for the business or workplace in terms of financial loss and these are worth mentioning, especially if the management is questioning your choice of training topics (see Chapter 5: Consequences and Legal Implications).

Plenary: Collate all the consequences both for the individual and the organization. The two major issues here are the moral issues and the financial ones.

Expected outcomes: The participants will probably list a whole range of emotional, physical and financial consequences for the victim. Don't forget that the recipient's family and friends may also suffer. Lastly list the consequences for the organization which are largely financial due to staff turnover, lost productivity, waste of paid work time, low morale and possible compensation claims and tribunal costs.

1.00 Lunch

1.45 Activity Five: Countering the myths and misconceptions of sexual harassment

Organization: I usually ask the participants to get into twos or threes and I give them some of the examples of the myths they are likely to encounter (they are taken from Chapter 9: Countering Myths and Misconceptions). I ask them to discuss some of the statements and to imagine that they are confronted, professionally, with a person making these comments. The task is to work out a suitable reply of an educative nature to convince the speaker that the statement is inaccurate, biased or plain wrong.

Time: I allow the participants 20 minutes to discuss this activity and a further 20 minutes for a whole-group discussion and to hear what they have decided to say.

Aims: The aim is to find educational responses, not sarcastic witticisms, put downs, angry retorts or dismissive gestures. Remember as a manager of this organization you will need to set an example. It will be of no value if you either just listen to, but remain silent about, sexist comments or are part of the ethos which perpetuates myths and misconceptions about sexual harassment.

Martin Luther King said about racism that if you were not part of the solution, then you were part of the problem. This, I think, applies equally well to sexism. To stand back and see a person being sexually harassed and not to say something directly to the harasser, to allow, by silence or default, sexist jokes to be told in the general office, to be part of the culture which says that sexual harassment is a women's issue only, to turn your back on pats and hugs which are making someone uncomfortable, is to be part of the problem.

Plenary: Once the managers have spent some time discussing the possible answers or writing down what to say, I invite them either to talk about any that they found especially difficult or to share some of the answers with us.

Expected outcomes: This session is usually quite a good one for discussion and for beginning to look at strategies for stopping and preventing sexual harassment, and its practical value is appreciated.

2.30 Activity Six: A grievance procedure

Organization: This session is designed to present to the managers a grievance procedure for the organization. You may wish to make overheads of the grievance procedure (see Chapter 7: A Grievance Procedure).

Time: This activity takes about 30 minutes.

Aims: The managers need to be familiar with their responsibilities with respect to a case of harassment. They need to know what to do, how to respond, and the procedure to be adopted if a case of harassment is brought by an employee.

3.00 Tea

3.15 Activity Seven: The role of the managers

Organization: In small groups ask the managers to decide on ten proactive things they can do to counter sexual harassment in this organization, their section/office/team (see Chapter 11: The Role of Management).

Time: Give the small groups about 20 minutes to decide on their roles, what they can do and how they are going to do it.

Aims: To have the managers consider in real terms what they can contribute to the organization's policy of countering sexual harassment.

Plenary: Collate and discuss their suggestions. Add more of your own if necessary (see Chapter 11: The Role of Management).

3.45 Activity Eight : The anxious workplace

Organization: In small groups ask the managers to look at the scenarios described in Chapter 8: Countering the Sceptics. Ask them what responses they would make to the four employees described on page 65, given what they now know about sexual harassment and the difficulties with it, the denial of some employees yet the need to counter it.

Time: Give the small groups about 20 minutes to decide on their responses.

Aims: To have the managers consider in real terms how they would defuse the anxious workplace.

Plenary: As a whole group discuss their suggestions. Give them the responses as described in Chapter 8: Countering the Sceptics.

4.15 Activity Nine: Sexual harassment and the law

Organization: A presenter will have to give an overview of the Sex Discrimination Act (1975). It will probably be necessary to make overheads of the relevant clauses.

Time: I spend approximately 30 minutes on this section, just slowly working through the laws so that the participants understand the legal framework.

Aims: For managers to understand their legal responsibilities with regard to liability, to encourage them to take the initiative in countering sexual harassment in the workplace and to realize that some kinds of sexual harassment, which constitute sex discrimination, are unlawful.

4.45 Questions and feedback
5.00 Close

BIBLIOGRAPHY

References

Anderson, R., Brown, J. and Campbell E. (1993) *Aspects of Sex Discrimination within the Police Service in England and Wales.* Hampshire Constabulary. Crown Copyright (Home Office).

British Broadcasting Corporation (1993) *Making Advances: Sexual Harassment in the Workplace.* London: BBC Enterprise Videos.

Farley, L. (1978 rpt 1980) *Sexual Shakedown. The Sexual Harassment of Women on the Job.* New York: Warner Books.

Hellerstein, E.O., Hume, L.P. and Offen, K.M. (1981) (eds) *Victorian Women. A Documentary Account of Women's Lives in Nineteenth-Century England, France, and the United States.* Stanford, California: Stanford University Press.

Herbert, C.M.H. (1993) *Countering Sexual Harassment: A Pack.* Cambridge: Daniels Publishing.

Hopkins, J. (1984) (ed.) *Perspectives on Rape and Sexual Assault.* London: Harper/Row.

Lowe, M. (1984) 'The role of the judiciary in the failure of the Sexual Offences (Amendment) Act to improve the treatment of the rape victim', in Hopkins (1984).

National Union of Teachers (1992) *Harassment: a Union Issue.* London: NUT .

Rousseau, J-J. (1762 rpt 1984) *Emile.* London: John Dent.

Rubenstein, M. (1989) *The Dignity of Women at Work. Parts i - iii.* Brussels: Commission of the European Communities.

Sedley A. and Benn M. (1984) *Sexual Harassment at Work.* London: The National Council for Civil Liberties.

Swann, J. (1992) *Girls, Boys and Language.* Oxford: Blackwell.

Trades Union Congress (1983) *Sexual Harassment of Women at Work: A Study from West Yorkshire/Leeds Trade Union and Community Research and Information Centre.* London: Trades Union Congress.

Trades Union Congress (ed) (1991) (revised) *Sexual Harassment at Work: TUC guidelines*. London: TUC.

WASH (1990) *Sexual Harassment of Women in the Workplace: A Guide to Legal Action*. London: WASH.

Further reading

Department of Employment (1992) *Sexual Harassment in the Workplace: a guide for employers*. ISCO, The Paddocks, Frizinghall, Bradford BD9 4HD.

Department of Employment (1992) *Sexual Harassment in the Workplace: the facts employees should know*. ISCO, The Paddocks, Frizinghall, Bradford BD9 4HD.

Dziech, B.W. and Weiner, L. (1984) *The Lecherous Professor; Sexual Harassment on Campus*. Boston: Beacon Press.

Grabrucker, M. (1988) *There's a Good Girl: Gender stereotyping in the first three years of life: A Diary*. London: The Women's Press.

Hadjifotou, N. (1983) *Women and Harassment at Work*. London: Pluto Press.

Hall, C. (1992) *White, Male and Middle Class*. Cambridge: Polity Press.

Hanmer, J. and Maynard, M. (1987) (eds) *Women, Violence and Social Control*. Basingstoke: Macmillan.

Hanmer, J. and Saunders, S. (1984) *Well Founded Fear. A Community Study of Violence to Women*. London: Hutchinson in association with The Explorations in Feminism Collective.

Herbert, C.M.H. (1989) *Talking of Silence: the Sexual Harassment of Schoolgirls*. London: Falmer Press.

Herbert, C.M.H. (1992) *Sexual Harassment in Schools: A Guide for Teachers*. London: David Fulton Publishers.

MacKinnon, C.A. (1979) *Sexual Harassment of Working Women*. New Haven: Yale University Press.

Mahony, P. (1984) *Schools for the Boys: Coeducation Reassessed*. London: Hutchinson in association with The Explorations in Feminism Collective.

Millett, K. (1970 rpt 1983) *Sexual Politics*. London: Virago Press.

NASUWT (1990) *Sexual Harassment: Action for Equality*. Birmingham: NASUWT.

Nicholson, J. (1984) *Men and Women. How different are they?* Oxford: Oxford University Press.

Read, J. (1988) *The Equal Opportunities Book*. London: Interchange Books.

Read, S. (1982) *Sexual Harassment at Work*. London: Hamlyn.

Rubenstein M. (1989) *Preventing and Remedying Sexual Harassment at Work*. London: Industrial Relations Services.

Seager, J. and Olson, A. (1986) *Women in the World; An International Atlas*. London: Pan Books.

Sumrall A.C. and Taylor D. (eds) (1992) *Sexual Harassment: Women Speak Out*. California: Crossing Press.

Walby S. (ed.) (1988) *Gender Segregation at Work*. Milton Keynes: Open University Press.

Wise, S. and Stanley, L. (1987) *Georgie Porgie: Sexual Harassment in Everyday Life*. London: Pandora Press.

USEFUL ADDRESSES

Carrie Herbert Consultancy: Rhadegund House, 49 New Square, Cambridge CB1 1EZ. Tel/fax: (0223) 66052.

Central Office of the Industrial Tribunals: 100 Southgate Street, Bury St Edmunds, Suffolk 1P33 2AQ. Tel: (0284) 762300.

City Centre: 32-35 Featherstone Street, London EC1Y 8QX. Tel: (071) 608 1338.

Employment Relations Advisory Services (ERAS): Clive Gillott, 5 Wilderspin Close, Girton, Cambridge CB3 0LZ. Tel: (0223) 510355. Fax: (0223) 510360

Equal Opportunities Commission: Overseas House, Quay Street, Manchester M3 3HN. Tel: (061) 833 9244.

Institute of Personnel Management: IPM House, Camp Road, Wimbledon, London SW19 4UX. Tel: (081) 946 9100. Fax: (081) 947 2570

National Associations of Citizens Advice Bureaux: 115 Pentonville Road, N1 9LZ. Tel: (071) 833 2181.

National Harassment Network: University of Central Lancashire, Preston PR1 2BR. Tel: (0772) 892253.

Personnel Advisory Services, (PAS): c/o Mrs Kate James, Central Administration Centre, Pinsley Orchard, Main Road, Long Hanborough, Witney, Oxfordshire, OX8 8JZ. Tel (0993) 881395. Fax (0993) 883495

Suzy Lamplugh Trust, National Charity for Personal Safety: 14 East Sheen Avenue, London SW14 8AS. Tel: (081) 392 1839. Fax (081) 392 1830.

Trades Union Congress: Gt. Russell Street, London WC1B 3LS. Tel: (071) 636 4030.

Women Against Sexual Harassment: 312 The Chandlery, 50 Westminster Bridge Road, London SE1 7QY. Tel: (071) 721 7592.

INDEX